JOBS

JOBS

HOW PEOPLE CREATE
THEIR OWN

William C. Ronco

Beacon Press

Boston

Beacon Press books are published under the auspices
of the Unitarian Universalist Association

Simultaneous publication in casebound and paperback editions

Published simultaneously in Canada by
Fitzhenry & Whiteside Limited, Toronto

Printed in the United States of America

(hardcover) 9 8 7 6 5 4 3 2 1
(paperback) 9 8 7 6 5 4 3 2 1

Library of Congress Cataloging in Publication Data

Ronco, William C
  Jobs: how people create their own.
  Includes index.
   1. Cooperation—United States—Case studies.
2. Work groups—United States—Case studies.　　3. Job
satisfaction—United States—Case studies.　　I. Title.
HD3444.R57　　　334'.6'0973　　　76-48525
ISBN 0-8070-2744-8
ISBN 0-8070-2745-6 (pbk.)

To my parents

Contents

What This
Book
Is About

The most important thing about the woodworking group, a member told me, was that it enabled her and the other members to "do the kind of work we want to do." At first I didn't understand what she meant—after all, wasn't woodworking the kind of work they wanted to do, and wasn't all woodworking pretty much the same in any kind of group? As I watched the group, though, and found out more about it, the meaning of what she said became much clearer.

Some members lived for woodworking. They lavished attention on their pieces, and it was apparent that they would have difficulties in a work setting that didn't allow for that kind of personal involvement. Others were more concerned with the group's organization than with woodworking as such. They wanted to be able to change their work schedules frequently, to maintain a general schedule that traditionally organized firms would probably not accommodate.

I realized that the woodworking group had at root two driving forces: ownership and craftsmanship, and that both worked out in a complex way. Members of the group literally owned it. They had invested their money and time and could go out of their way to accommodate unorthodox demands because they were making those demands themselves. Also, underlying formal ownership was a more basic kind of ownership—their self-ownership, which they expressed and resolved in each decision they made.

The group exercised craftsmanship in their wood-working, but they also crafted the nature of their work. They designed their schedules, they carefully shaped their relationships with clients and with each other, they refined their own understanding of what the work meant to them.

This book is about work arrangements that, like the woodworking group's, combine ownership with crafts-manship of the work, that enable people to "do the kind of work we want to do." Some people are able to find such work in the traditionally organized workplace, but many cannot. The evolving nature of the workplace is not helping matters—it seems work is defined in an increasingly limited way, and that definition is spreading to all types of work, even those once assumed immune to such limitation. Chapter 1 explores the emerging monolithic design of the traditional workplace and details the concept of owning and designing one's own work.

Chapter 2 examines an area in which one would expect to find an extreme sort of work ownership and design—the professional art and crafts "scene." The chapter describes the work of various artisans and the kinds of organizations that promote that work. Chapter 3 describes the trend to bureaucratization in the profes-sions, where "meaningful work" traditionally found a stronghold. It reports on emerging alternative organi-zations for work in law, architecture, and public elemen-tary education. Chapter 4 focuses on a number of businesses that have been organized to meet more readily the needs of their owner-members. Generalizing from the text, concluding notes briefly suggest a framework for understanding the organization of alternative work organizations and outline policy to support them.

I had a great deal of help in writing this book, and I am most grateful for it. The people who gave me their time in interviews were most helpful, opening up in ways that surprised me and taught me a great deal. I was also fortunate to have received help in the form of material support from the Bemis Foundation, through the Laboratory of Architecture and Planning at M.I.T.

My teachers and colleagues also provided significant help, especially in formulating the arguments of the book and making them clear. Members of the faculty of the Department of Urban Studies and Planning at M.I.T., Gary Marx, Lisa Peattie, and Donald Schon, spent many hours with me in this cause. My friends John Case, Andrew Hahn, and Peter Linkow, my wife, Wilma Lilley Ronco, and my parents, Donald and Norma Bang (to whom this book is dedicated) also were most helpful in every aspect of preparing the manuscript.

W.R.

CHAPTER ONE

"The Kind of
Work We
Want to Do"

The incredible din of the woodworking machinery
might as well be perfect silence for all it affects him.
He does not pause, hesitate, or even avert his gaze but
continues unwaveringly to brush the table off, peering
beneath sawdust-flecked eyelids with intense admira-
tion and respect. For its part, the table responds well,
revealing complex weavings of cleanly textured grain
beneath the sawdust he sweeps away. In the background, the clatter of machinery diminishes slowly as
the other members of the group stop their work to pre-
pare for lunch.

Though there seems to be no more sawdust he continues to brush, nodding to the others as they pass by.
Some of them stop for a moment and join him in looking
at the table, surveying and appraising it quickly before
moving on to the refrigerator to get their lunch. Some
leave to pick up a take-out order from a nearby Chinese
restaurant. Propping brown-bag lunches on available
outcroppings of wood or tools, those that remain pull
up stools around the table. Occasionally they glance
at the table, then back at the work they have left in the

other areas of the shop: cabinets, chairs, other tables, and yet indeterminate, apparently random assemblages of wood.

The brown-baggers begin eating, prompting him to reluctantly brush off the table with yet a few more strokes. With a parting glance over his shoulder, he retrieves his lunch, the last in the refrigerator, and returns to join the others. Carefully placing a T square in a wall rack, he clears a space to sit down.

The conversation focuses on a cabinet at the opposite end of the shop, and he joins in with a few critical comments about what could be done to make the cabinet stronger. A few of the others disagree, and the discussion moves on quickly through a review of everyone's experience and opinions.

The conversation is loose, yet serious, drawing a bit from everyone and pointing out a unique feature of this work group: it has no boss. Further, people criticize each other's work and no one gets upset; people change their work assignments themselves in the midst of the lunch discussion, trading work, and in some cases putting it off; people are involved and even enthusiastic. This woodworking group is in fact quite different from most woodworking companies—it is run and owned by its members, about a dozen of them.

The group fares well in the competitive local market. It specializes in custom work and usually has enough work to keep its members as busy as they choose to be. When the flow of custom work slows down, they subcontract to furniture stores and produce stock items that bear store labels. But the members of the group sometimes choose not to take on stock item work, opting instead for developing their own interests at a reduced rate of return or possibly even choosing idleness. Because it is run by its members, the group functions first to meet members' needs. Often, their primary needs are financial, and the group provides a vehicle for earning money: contacting, contracting, and carrying out the work in a comfortable environment. Usually, though, the need for money is compromised by needs for less tangible concerns, such as doing the work in a particular way, or learning to do a particular kind of work.

Ideally, everyone in the group is interested in the available work and the group takes on as much work as members want. If the available work is uninteresting, members take on as much as they must. The crucial point is that the organization responds to their needs quickly, and this response helps make the work more satisfying. Equally important, members design the tasks and decide who will do what and when. They own the firm and share in its profits.

Reflecting its members' diverse interests, the woodworking group flexes and changes in response to changing environments and internal needs. In times when all members face financial difficulty, the whole group takes on extra work, possibly of the variety scorned in better times. More typically, the organization responds to members' differing levels of need, supplying fulltime shop work for those who want it and a network of job leads and contacts for outdoor carpentry or similarly flexible kinds of work. Members usually move from work in the shop to work outside, depending on their financial needs, what work is available, and their current interests in varying kinds of work, though not necessarily in that order. (Interest in porch-building escalates significantly on sunny days.)

Some members of the group seldom appear in the shop at all, and some people who are not members but merely friends and acquaintances earn a living from the same network through referrals and informal contacts. This "shadow group," an informal network, uses the woodworking group as a clearinghouse and keeps the whole group abreast of developments elsewhere in the trade.

A member of the group pointed out: "One of the motivations for starting the group was that we wanted to do the kind of work we wanted to do." She emphasized the last seven words. "The kind of work we wanted to do" means for some of the members being able to devote more time to the pursuit of craftsmanship than a traditional shop would allow, or to approach the work as a learning event. Others are more drawn to the arrangement than to the content of the work, making good use of the group's flexible hours, days and weeks. The kind of work most members want to do changes, as they change, and the most important aspect of the group is that it changes along with them. Members of the woodworking group design their work with as much or perhaps even more care as they take with their tables.

OTHER GROUPS: A DIVERSITY

The organizing principles of the woodworking group seem well suited to its craft. It is easy to imagine other groups organized similarly for other crafts and trades, but not so easy to conceive of more complex kinds of work indigenously organized for workers' autonomy and control. Yet examples exist for a wide range of work, including architecture and law firms, public schools, retail stores and restaurants, even offices and factories.

Some resemble the part of the woodworking group that works in the shop but others look more like its informal network, or a combination of the two. International Group Plans, a Washington, D.C., insurance company, attempts to involve all its 350 employees in the ownership and management of the company. The teachers in the McCarthy-Towne School (Acton, Massachusetts) run the school, determining curriculum, discipline, and personnel policies, and establishing a uniform philosophy for the school. (The school, the insurance company, and many other of the organizations mentioned in this chapter are described in detail in the latter part of the book.)

Co-operatives formed by farmers and fishermen function much like the woodworking group's network, assisting members with sales and marketing to enable them to pursue their work interests with minimal interference. Often these networks center around an individual or a group whose job is making the network work. A woman who runs a gallery in a small home helps make it easier for local craftspeople to ply their trade and provides herself with interesting work as well. Guilds and co-ops of craftsmen operate similarly, providing diverse supports for craftsmen, offering advice on finances and sales and lending moral support.

Craftspeople themselves comprise a growing community of laborers characterized by their own design of their own work. They do not approach their work as a given, but engage actively in designing, defining, and redesigning it as they see fit.

Homesteading and self-sufficient farming in rural areas broach the issue of work as part of a larger redesign of living, attempting to break down some of the barriers between work and the rest of life. Homesteaders live sparsely, off the land as much as possible, and work on projects for themselves that have little to do with monetary exchange.

As in the woodworking group, these arrangements grant members control over the work they do. In varying degrees they participate directly in management.

The groups offer a measure of stability, vitality, and psychological support for individuals who want it.

This book focuses on the smaller kinds of these organizations (most have about a dozen active members), kinds people can easily initiate, create, and design by themselves or with a group of friends or colleagues. Larger organizations, like the worker-run plywood companies of the Pacific Northwest and the farming co-ops of Southern California, are important and have received a measure of attention from various analysts. The journal *Working Papers* has run articles on a take-over of a factory by its workers, the plywood companies, and California farming co-ops.

Though they may be more significant economically, larger organizations can't allow for the flexibility, innovation, and promotion of personal expression in work that smaller groups can cultivate. There are fewer people to satisfy in smaller groups and thus a potential to satisfy them better. Following E. F. Schumacher's dictum that *Small Is Beautiful*[1] for many economic endeavors, this book explores in detail how small groups strive to make work a beautiful experience for their members.

The co-operative, nonhierarchical form is rare and important among organizations. Apart from how they may influence the successful design of work, work co-ops and collectives are interesting purely as organizations because of their smallness, their high level of internal communication, and their concern for introspection.

It is difficult to get an exact measure of how many people design their own work and how that number might be changing, but existing support networks, rural migration patterns, and architectural trends provide some insights:

*Networks that support work collectives and work co-ops exist in several major cities, each listing between twenty and forty organizations that cover, like those in this book, a range of kinds of work and kinds of organizations. Some of these networks, like Boston's Vocations for Social Change and Washington, D.C.'s Strongforce, are marked by very high levels of activity. Vocations for Social Change carries on a career counseling operation and publishes the popular *Peoples' Yellow Pages.* Strongforce has received substantial funding from the National Institute for Mental Health to publish, along with its newsletters, a set of training manuals on worker-run businesses.

*One view[2] of the census figures showing a decrease in urban metropolitan population and a population increase in rural areas suggests a "move back to the country" by a wave of disgruntled city dwellers seeking their (not always figurative) forty acres and a mule. A recent *Money* magazine article details the various work experiences of a chiropractor-turned-dairy-farmer, a salesman-turned-wheat farmer, a business products demonstrator-turned-craftsman, and so on.

*Architectural trends are yet another clue: more and more commercial enterprises are being built to host many small businesses rather than a few large ones. This sensitivity to small business can come from only one source—the existence of a market of renters for these spaces. The small business umbrellas may be an attempt to link boutique marketing with a permanent crafts fair. In several Massachusetts sites, developers have carved up the shell of a bankrupt discount store (they dot the national landscape, victims of the last economic crunch) into a set of small spaces for small businesses.

*The statistics on self-employment and small businesses are very relevant here, but they include many distorting factors. For example, "small" in some small business statistics may mean any enterprise capitalized at less than a million dollars.

Businesses designated as self-employment, however, don't accurately describe the work environment. Some self-employed people work alone in an attic, others may work side by side with their employees. That the work environments discussed here do not appear in mainstream information sources should not be a surprise —the groups simply do not fit within existing categories.

WORK PEOPLE DESIGN FOR THEMSELVES

The difference between work people design for themselves and predesigned work is much like the difference between a house people design for themselves and one they select from the available market. Like designing one's house, designing one's work is qualitatively different from selecting from an available range. In both cases the impetus to design arises out of dissatisfaction with what is available. What the market offers is often too small, too big, too expensive, too demanding, too narrow. The product the market offers may be perfectly satisfactory, but people simply want to engage themselves in the process of design. The impetus for work people design for themselves can be traced to both dissatisfaction with available arrangements and the thrill of design, with the push of the former and the pull of the latter emerging as powerful forces and the boundary between each sometimes indistinguishable.

The push of ownership also suggests a crucial shortcoming of the comparison between designing one's work. The concept of design suggests the cognitive complexity of the process, but belies the depth of emotional attachment involved. Designing one's own work is not a task coolly carried out but boldly asserted and wrapped up in emotion.

OWNERSHIP

The mentality of "bossism" can be brutalizing for workers in high- as well as low-paying jobs and can be a prime incentive for inspiring people to become their own bosses. Part of the problem of working for another ("appropriated labor," the economists call it) is the knowledge that the fruits of one's labors are benefiting someone else, a bitter pill to swallow if that someone else is not somebody a worker wishes to benefit.

The woman who operates the art gallery out of her home assured me "It's not much, but it's mine. Working for other people, whom I didn't like in the first place, so they could earn money off me, was too much to bear. Quitting made me ecstatic even if it will never make me rich."

International Group Plans (an insurance company in Washington, D.C.) maintains an arrangement that splits its ownership in half between its workers and its clients. The actual stock is held in trust and a share of its value allocated to employee-members only when they leave the company. All employee-members, apart from rank or seniority, own an equal share, and the value has reached substantial levels. A clerk who had been there for two years received $3,600 when she moved out of the area. Client ownership helps ensure that the company represents clients' needs well and has convinced some fairly large accounts to patronize (thereby literally buying into) the company.

Ownership in smaller groups is often expressed in ways that help members affirm their humanity and integrity. A woman in the Common Stock restaurant in Waltham, Massachusetts, explained: "Some customers don't know. They snap their fingers and expect you to hurry up and drop everything. Then when you get there, they give you a hard time. I usually try and reason things through with them, and we usually end up friends. After all, most people basically want to be nice. But when you hit the ones that don't, you can say, and I have a few times, 'If you don't like it, leave.' Then when they ask to speak to the owner, I tell them, 'I am the owner.'

"There are some nice things about being an owner, too. Like when the delivery people come in and ask to speak to the owner we tell them any one of us is as good as the other. One of the best things is when a customer asks if the apple pie is good and I say, 'It sure is. I made it.' Then too, every once in a while I notice myself wiping off a fingerprint or picking up a speck of dust and taking pride in it all."

Ownership is often an important beginning to work people design for themselves, an expression not only of owning a business but also of owning oneself. Such ownership alone may be what people strive for and find satisfying. This kind of feeling is at the crux of entrepreneuring, self-employed shopkeeping, self-management in larger groups, and Mother Earth–type self-sufficiency in the boondocks. This is the feeling that comes with making a declaration of independence. It's a heady feeling that, for many, substitutes well for a more intense exploration of meaning within the work.

Ownership can also be a powerful emotional issue, and it is helpful to realize that many of the individuals and groups described in this book have as their base not a cool, cognitive rationale but a highly emotional reaction to some intolerable situation. The emotional base of many of the arrangements and the diversity of needs with which people approach them lead to some sharp contrasts.

Some operate in the small business mode; there are blue-jeaned, laconic craftsmen doing pottery or weaving whose profit-and-loss statements would make Adam Smith proud. Others, feeling the control of their work, attempt to redefine it and may place doing traditional business at the bottom of their priorities while devoting the bulk of their energy to extracting as much satisfaction as possible from the work.

The diversity of efforts and their emotional overtones may contribute to the misleading notion that they are somehow not serious, that their members are playing at work. In articles on the groups and individuals that appear in the feature sections of Sunday newspapers, people inevitably are depicted as characters, eccentrics, harmless but not quite real. The message between the lines points to cute but harmless anachronisms, but nothing worthy of serious consideration.

THE IMPORTANCE OF WORK

Work that people design for themselves demands more serious consideration than it usually gets because work itself is a serious matter and because the prevailing shape of work seems headed in a way that highlights the importance of small, autonomous, self-designed arrangements.

In his preface to *Work in America*, Eliot Richardson pointedly underscored what many social scientists and policymakers have long believed: "However deeply we cared in the past, we never really understood the importance, the meaning and the reach of work."[3] The text bore his statement out and reinforced it, citing numerous primary sources documenting the importance of work for individuals' longevity, physical health and mental health,[4]

The framework for the meaning of work in an individual's mental health assigns work "a crucial and perhaps unparalleled role in the formation of self-esteem, identity, and a sense of order."[5] Specific studies cited by *Work in America* to fill in this framework feature Arthur Kornhauser's *Mental Health of the Industrial Worker*.[6] Kornhauser's work is now nearly twenty years old but the picture it presents is generally viewed as an underestimate of the current problems. Kornhauser's findings included correlations between job satisfaction and absenteeism and feelings of helplessness, withdrawal, alienation, and pessimism.

Other studies of work and mental health offer a similar split in findings between such tangible measures as absenteeism and more general clinical observations such as feelings of helplessness. Perhaps the most striking findings relate work to alcoholism, drug abuse, and suicide.[7] In a different but equally chilling, vein, some psychologists advance the notion that people cope or adjust downward to pathological situations, retreating and withdrawing in order to come to terms with the demands of the organizations they confront.

Work also has meaning for society beyond its importance to individuals. A Canadian study argued that "a restrictive and confining work environment is not easily dropped at the mill gates,"[8] but is also felt in the family and community. An experiment in participatory job redesign observed that its subjects became more active in community activities.[9]

The British theorist G. D. H. Cole argued that "Political democracy must be completed by democracy in the workshop,"[10] pointing out a particularly important role for the organization of work in a democratic society. Research on participation[11] indicates that affiliation with associations in which an opportunity exists for people to take an active role relates to generally increased political activity. Democratically organized workplaces afford opportunities for such active roles and thus should foster increased political activity.

INCREASING BUREAUCRACY IN THE WORKPLACE

The impetus to design one's own work arises at least in part from the predominant shape of available, predesigned work, a shape that seems best described as a monolith. Some people flee from the monolith for something completely different, whereas others persevere and try to do the work they started out to do in a way more suited to them. What they are all acting against is the narrow, restricted shape which is increasingly is becoming the norm for work arrangements. It is possible for people to design some elements of all sorts of work, but a strong trend seems to be reducing the number and reach of elements that could be under worker's control.

The emerging organization of work seems to conflict directly with the prospects for a variety of arrangements and meanings for work, with trends indicating fewer opportunities for democracy in the workshop, instead increasing bureaucratization, job segmentation, and a uniformly narrow definition of work.

The deeply felt implications of bureaucratization are mirrored in entire dating book at least as far as Chaplin's film *Modern Times* and more recently in Studs Terkel's *Working* and Joseph Heller's *Something Happened*. All depict a workplace that has grown beyond humanly manageable proportions into a Frankenstein that turns with a vengeance on its creators.

Lest all this seem a bit too dramatic, several kinds of

empirical evidence regarding the size of workplaces
underscore its seriousness:

> There has been a dramatic decrease of small, independent
> enterprises and an increase of the domination of large corpo-
> rations and government in the workplace. Some 2 percent
> of industrial units account for 50.6 percent of all industrial
> employees.[12]
> Over half the workforce is employed in firms that have
> more than 100 employees.[13]
> The trend to bigness is true not just of industry and manu-
> facturing, but the professions as well.[14]
> Self-employed people account for about 8 percent of the
> workforce.[15]

Perhaps more significant than the size of workplaces
is the almost inevitable observation that serious changes
in the nature of the work accompany such growth,
changes that nearly always tend to segment jobs, to
break them down into manageable pieces. Sociologist
Peter L. Berger notes:

> there exist today situations of assembly-line medicine,
> assembly-line law, and even assembly-line research, with
> physicians, lawyers and scientists attached to a small frag-
> ment of the overall work process very much as the auto-
> mobile worker is to "his" place in the assembly line.[16]

Work in America echoes this observation, focusing
on bureaucracies' organization of work to maximize
predictability and control, creating for workers a
"tyranny of the bureaucracy."[17]

The irony, perhaps better viewed as a tragedy, in the
bureaucratization of work is that it represents so much
energy, so much potential and knowledge. The insightful economist Tibor Scitovsky has noted that

Proportion of Workers by Type of Work and Size of Firm, 1972

(County Business Patterns, 1972, Table 1C)

Employed in agriculture		4.3%
Self-employed		6.5
Non-agricultural, private employees		72.9
SIZE OF FIRM		
1–3 employees	3.7%	
4–7 employees	4.8	
8–19 employees	9.0	
20–49 employees	10.7	
50–99 employees	7.7	
100–499 employees	17.0	
500+ employees	18.2	
not known	1.9	
Government employees		16.3
		100.0%

> Modern technology creates great possibilities, but it also
> pushes us toward standardization and uniformity, both
> of which inhibit our ability to exploit the possibilities it
> creates.[18]

Technology often inhibits human expression, ignoring
consideration for human input. People who design
their own work often strike out most visibly against
standardization and uniformity, attempting to establish
a more personal kind of work.

Individuals working in large organizations (or even
in professions, as Berger points out) face a growing
number of jobs that don't allow for much input. Iron-
ically, the trend in job bureaucratization that has
reduced the scope of workers' input is neatly matched
by a trend of increasing education that leads workers
to expect to have greater input. One study cited using
one's intellectual facilities on the job as "the prime
incentive" for young workers, but the bureaucratization
does not allow for it.[19] Bureaucratized jobs make it
increasingly difficult for people who wish to approach
their work as a craft. The plight of an autoworker who
wants to view his bolting operation (one minute—ten
rivets) as a craft is tragic indeed.

Defining work narrowly also limits the amount of
self-identification people can derive from their work.
Peter Berger believes that in the past people's work
more powerfully shaped their identity than it does today
(e.g., a person *was* a blacksmith). Though this kind of
identification could not always be linked to esteem, it
at least provided an individual with a unified sense of
self unattainable through more narrow job descriptions.
People who design their own work can derive from the
act of design a measure of this kind of self-identification,
much as can people who design their own home. The
toymaker who exults, "I *am* Gepetto" is not kidding.

The act of design is itself an expression of oneself in any work that people structure for themselves.

Bureaucratized work not only defines work narrowly but also depersonalizes it, as graphically depicted in a national public opinion poll.[20] Seventy-six percent of the respondents who were working indicated that they had a supervisor to whom they were directly responsible, and that 77 percent of those supervisors were directly responsible to another supervisor. Only 18 percent of the respondents who were working had a supervisor not directly responsible to another supervisor, and only 22 percent of the working respondents had no supervisor.

The presence of a supervisor is of course inconclusive evidence for the limitation of a worker's autonomy on the job, but it is at least a general approximation of work settings. More significant perhaps is the supervisor-of-supervisor issue, which indicates layers of bureaucracy and control removed from the worker and which seems to exist in significant amounts. It is the supervisors and their supervisors who have most to do with the structuring of control and knowledge, with the depersonalization of work.

Layers of supervision and bureaucracy in monolithic work arrangements can be oppressive not only because of what they may do to workers, but simply because they are there. Even a benevolent bureaucracy can be difficult to deal with and impossible to grasp in personal terms. As bureaucratized work increasingly evolves as the only game in town, the more personal arrangements people design for themselves can take meaning even merely in their smallness.

People who design work for themselves often relish the more personal aspects, the same aspects that bureaucratized work tries to wash away. In work that people design for themselves, interactions with customers and clients, wholesalers and colleagues, co-workers and co-owners may be cherished and celebrated rather than reduced to a bare minimum.

THE ELEMENTS OF DESIGN

Overall, work people design for themselves reflects a degree of personalization in many aspects, paying attention to a richness of human interests and enterprises given free rein. Office workers often personalize all possible aspects of their work: they arrange their desks with pictures and plants, taking a degree of care no less than that of any artist; they plot for weeks to get the chair, adding machine, or typewriter they want. These same instincts, given reach over a whole job, produce the work that people design for themselves.

The range of what may be designed is partly in the work itself, in its structure, in the speed and order in which it is approached, in the degree of feeling that may be invested in it, in the expectations for financial reward attached to it, in the choice of whether to do it or not. Also subject to design are the environs of the work, especially the environs of human relations between workers and the "outside world," workers and their families, and workers in their own groupings. People who design their own work often take great care with both aspects that are part of the work and aspects of the work's environs.

Designing the Process of Work. On their own or in groups, people who design their own work approach it largely at their own pace. Professors who like to keep their own hours call this "lack of labor discipline,"[21] but it may involve a very high degree of discipline. It's just that the discipline of self-initiation is self-imposed, and for some people that makes it tolerable and sometimes even enjoyable. People working on their own or in organizations like the work co-ops and collectives set the terms of their own discipline and avoid the material and psychological subjection of working for another.

Given the ability to vary pace, some groups gear it to the particular projects they happen to be working on. The woodworking group, for example, works overtime on a project until it is completed. Exhausted, they then rest until they have the energy to begin another piece of work. Other craftspeople vary their pace in much the same way, giving themselves over to a massive production effort for an exhibit or in response to the creative mandate of a piece they are working on. For some, varying the pace may mean simply slowing it down, which may be important to enable them to do it in a way they feel it should be done.

Groups of people that design their own work usually approach the issue of pace in their schedule, which may mean giving up some spontaneity and impulse in exchange for the predictability necessary to keep a complex operation intact. Groups may have schedules that allow for large amounts of variability in the amount and placement of members' time commitments. At a weekly meeting, members will select their hours for the following week with an eye to filling the group's base requirements. Members of a restaurant collective, for example, fill in their whole schedules only after they have selected the day managers from among the group who coordinate the restaurant for a day each week.

Aside from pace, people also often design the structure and course of the work. A craftsperson producing ten quilts may do each quilt as a whole or break the work down, doing at once the cutting, the matching, the stitching for all ten. Usually groups and individuals design the structure of the work to mix these approaches, giving themselves over for a while to "production" work that breaks the work down into little pieces and then putting them into "whole work" approaches that give a greater sense of the product. Some groups, like a law collective, go out of their way to always enable workers to do a "whole" job.

Often there is a compromise in productivity that comes with approaching the work as an integrated whole, and in resolving that compromise people can meet their changing needs and interests. In a hungry month an artist can turn out a lot of saleable watercolors that don't really move her but at least pay the bills so she can explore abstracts the following month.

Many people are very conscious of their development —their learning, increased proficiency and skill—and they may thus need more time to experiment than to produce stock items. It may be in the interest—in both the personal-development and hard-nosed senses—for a lawyer in a law commune to take on an esoteric case that provides a challenge rather than handle a few well-paying divorces in the same time period.

Knowledge, Mastery, Control. In resolving the compromises of money versus personal expression, people who design their own work usually touch on three themes: knowledge, mastery and control. Harry Braverman identifies the role of knowledge in work as crucial.[22] He reviews Frederick Taylor's classic "scientific management," contending that Taylor's major thrust (the influence of which, he contends, underlies the trend to bureaucratization sketched out above) has to do with the centralization of knowledge in the hands of managers and the removal of knowledge from workers.

Under scientific management, jobs were broken down so that each worker was responsible for only a small task of the production process. While workers themselves formerly used their own knowledge to devise and execute this breakdown (or design) of a job, only managers did so under scientific management. The scope of a worker's work shrank from job to task and the application of his knowledge was required in ever decreasing areas. Conversely, the manager's knowledge was called upon to account for the work outside the parameters of the worker's input. Managers, using their centralized knowledge, gained significantly greater control over the overall process of production.

The knowledge of the whole job was broken up, dispersed in its execution among many workers, but focused in its control by management. Braverman terms this the "separation of conception from execution."[23] His observations on the trend to bureaucratization are anchored in the utility of this separation for managers and the expansion of the simple separation into division and hostility.[24] Workers without a sense of the whole job are subject to exploitation and manipulation with the knowledge that managers monopolize.

There are some additional facets of the knowledge issue from the workers' side, having to do more with despair and frustration than hostility. Segmenting a job into tasks has multiple effects—it breaks one diverse piece of work into several not so diverse pieces, thereby losing some of the interest inherent in diversity. Interest in a job does not end with variety, though. Job segmentation also breaks up the *cumulative* effect of diversity on work. A diverse job consists not merely of the pieces of the job, but also of the way they are put together, and it is exactly that putting together that scientific management breaks apart.

The act of breaking a job apart in itself communicates significantly to workers, making it clear that their claim over a task is at a bare minimum. This in turn minimizes the amount of attachment they can have to the work while it maximizes the strength of the message that they are laboring for someone else—the manger who has segmented his job also very clearly appropriates his labor.

In designing one's own work, it is possible and even common to end up with an overall work organization that segments jobs that break up the knowledge of the work. However, there is a great deal of difference between segmented work that people have arranged for themselves, that is open to change and redesign, and segmented work that is given and unalterable.

Knowledge used in work is closely related to mastery and control, but these issues warrant some examination on their own. Control, as in the control that managers get as a result of scientific management, is also the element of work that researchers[25] single out as being a key, perhaps the most important, to job satisfaction. The control over one's immediate work environment makes it possible for a worker to invest himself more fully in the work process and expands the degree and scope to which a worker's knowledge is utilized.

Such control could be viewed both as an application of knowledge and as a kind of knowledge in itself. In Braverman's terms, this control enables a worker to reunite conception with execution. This reunification refutes the cornerstone of scientific management, that an "absolute necessity for management[is] the dictation to the worker of the precise manner in which the work is to be performed."[26]

Mastery also bears exploration here since it is identified as an important element in the literature on adult ego development. One theorist contends: "the striving to master, to integrate, to make sense of experience is not one ego function among many but the essence of ego."[27] In this perspective, it is easy to see that the absence of such an opportunity to master in work, which occupies so much human time, would be frustrating and hinder ego development on a large scale.

The bureaucratization of work points to an increasingly smaller range of options for organizing work. And it's a range that seems to demand greater uniformity of commitment and to wreak havoc on the considerations of knowledge, mastery, and control. There is little room in bureaucratized work for either the dedicated craftsman seeking fulfillment through the work or for the home- and family-oriented person whose needs can't be met by work.

Restructuring work to alter the inputs of knowledge, mastery and control play out in a wide range of actual arrangements when people design their own work. Most typically, people design their own work to contrast with bureaucratized work, enabling themselves to readily adjust all stages of the work, to use of their knowledge in numerous chores. Craftspeople best exemplify the range of possibilities: some engage themselves in producing their raw materials and in dealing directly with customers at exhibitions while others prefer to concentrate on creative production, leaving sales to a gallery or an agent.

DESIGNING WORK FOR MULTIPLE MEANINGS

Restructuring work can be seen as an end in itself, but is better viewed as a result of a motivation to design work to reflect a range of multiple meanings. While bureaucratized work attempts to limit the range of possible meanings work can have, self-designed work tries to stretch the range, articulate its possibilities, and try them out. Articulation is more difficult than it sounds, largely because the possibility of more than a narrow range of definitions has been obscured by current practice—but several alternatives do exist.

People who want to express themselves in their work sometimes define that expression as political. They see their work as a medium for expressing their politics as much as (and sometimes more than) for expressing their art. These people are often doubly frustrated by bureaucratic work that constrains their creativity and inhibits the free exchange of their ideas.

One line of thought holds out work as a sort of biological imperative, a manifest destiny toward which human beings inevitably strive. Marx espoused this view and believed one of capitalism's tragedies to be the alienation of workers from their work. The authors of *Work in America* held a similar view, expressed at the beginning of their report around the issue of *homo faber*.[28] Proponents of this view see work as an art, perhaps referring to a view of work as a craft held over from days gone by.

The most eloquent references of the "work as art" view are products of an earlier, less self-conscious era. Roycroft—Elbert Hubbard's turn-of-the-century crafts co-op in East Aurora, New York—published a magazine, *The Philistine*,[29] and numerous other books and

pamphlets. They illuminated such views on work as
the following, which sometimes found their way into
the group's hand-tooled leather-covered publications:

"Life Without Industry Is Guilt—Industry Without Art
  Is Brutality"
"Blessed Is That Man Who Has Found His Work."
"The Curse of the World Is Joyless Labor"
"Art Is the Expression of Man's Joy in his Work."

People who design their own work in this era often do
so to capture the essence of the feeling expressed in
Hubbard's time. They design work to capture a bit of
art even if the work itself has nothing whatever to do
with fine art. There is unmistakably an element of art
in teaching at the public school run by its teachers, in
the practice of law in the law collective, in the everyday
business of the collectively run restaurant.

Some historians argue against the view that work is
a biological imperative, indicating that the "work as
art" perspective is more of a social quirk, and that
usually in history work was viewed as simple drudgery.
It may be that the nostalgic view of crafts had little to
do with historical reality and that craftsmen accounted
for only a small percentage of medieval workers, most
of whom were peasants. It seems that "making a living"
has often come to mean pursuit of one's interests
through the material rewards of work, and not its
practice or process. The issue of personal fulfillment
so dear to craftspeople of the current era does not seem
to enter the picture here at all, and the Protestant Ethic
of later years did little but eliminate the issue entirely.

During the Industrial Revolution, workers came into
the labor force not because of their love of work or in

response to their poverty, but to the newly developing idea that "gain" was something that everyone ought to do. "Acquisitiveness became a recognized virtue," one economic historian observes, helping to articulate the notion that the rewards of work are external to the work process.[30]

A concentrated version of this thought perhaps more influential for people who design their own work now is expressed in the predominant view of economists that work is to be viewed as a disutility, a necessary evil with which everyone must contend. This sentiment echoes the classic tradition of the Protestant Ethic that work "was holy and unpleasant, and that ideally it should be both."[31] Like mouthwash, work is a necessary evil to be submitted to, an inescapable and rather boring higher calling. Viewing work in this way, it is a fairly simple journey to the more recent viewpoint that work as an agent for humanism is a hopelessly quixotic platitude begging to be replaced by some concern for leisure. Against this backdrop, the current move to view work as an art emerges as a nearly perfectly radical idea.

Viewing work as a disutility leads fairly readily to a de-emphasis of concern for the way in which it is organized—why bother, after all, if people's interests are served elsewhere? Viewing work as an art may lead to an overemphasis on work organization and at least to a notion that everyone ought to be involved with work. Though mutually exclusive to some extent, both these views seem to shape currently popular conceptions of the social organization of work.

Somehow both views of work as art and work as disutility seem wrong in large part, but for opposite reasons. Work as art seems like a valuable ideal, but not practically realizable in the light of the prevailing social organization of work or necessarily appealing for every worker. Work as a disutility seems a practical response to the prevailing social organization of work but unmindful of its potential.

A view of work more representative of human interests and needs might begin with people, viewing work as an activity that different people approach with different needs and interests. For some people at some times of their lives, a de-emphasis of work provides an important path to the development of family and personal interests. For other people at other times, work is crucial as the medium of their emotional, intellectual, and creative involvement.

EXTERNAL ASPECTS OF WORK DESIGN

Besides all the aspects of the work itself that may be designed (its meaning, distribution of knowledge, pace, structure) a number of important aspects are external to the work such as the relationships between workers and the outside world and the relationships among workers. People who design their work often treat these relationships with the same kind of attention they pay to the work process itself. They try to personalize, to infuse humanity and personality into their work.

Relationships between individuals or groups and clients or customers, for example, are often designed to replace the objectivity of a formal relationship with a more personal approach. The professional collectives like the law collective and the architecture group do this by consciously trying to demystify their work,

to explain it in comprehensible terms. The work of
the collective becomes less intimidating and members
of the groups are seen as people rather than oracles.

Many individuals and groups also have more formal
teaching activities, such as the many craftspeople who
teach their craft. Some teach in very small, informal
groups to people who prevail on them for advice, others
offer formal classes and instruction. Some, like the
Mudflat group, evolve to place the teaching function
first. Formal and informal instruction help differen-
tiate the serious craftspeople and workers from their
customers, underscoring their expertise and cultivating
an appreciation for the work being done. This last element is extremely important, for like olives or brandy,
many of the products of people who design their work
are an acquired taste. A large part of the organizations'
teaching chore then, is the development of the taste.

There's a bit of education or appreciation in much
of the work that people design for themselves: in getting
used to "inn etiquette" at the Tamworth Inn as it differs
from staying in a motel, in learning about the plants
one buys at the Third Day, in students' learning the
relationship teachers expect of them at the McCarthy-
Towne School. Sometimes the education is good for
business but sometimes it's mostly a benefit for workers,
enabling them to carry a step further than themselves
their feeling for their work.

Besides the aspects of demystifying and education,
people who design their own work often attempt to
build into their relationships with others a much sim-
pler kind of personal statement. The owner-waiters/
waitresses at the Common Stock restaurant, for example, often pull up a chair and sit down when they take
a customer's order.

The extent to which workers design their relationships with each other usually exceeds the attention
they pay to the outside world. The work group may
well be the most important part of a work environment,
and members are often lavish in their concern for it.

CHAPTER TWO

Attention to Detail: The Lives and Work of Craftspeople

"A great deal of the joy of life consists in doing perfectly, or at least to the best of one's ability, everything which he attempts to do. There is a sense of satisfaction, a pride in surveying such a work—a work which is rounded, full, exact, complete in all its parts—which the superficial man who leaves his work in a slovenly, slipshod, half-finished condition, can never know. It is this conscientious completeness which turns work into art. The smallest thing, well done, becomes artistic." (William Matthews, in *Elbert Hubbard's Scrap Book*. New York: William H. Wise & Co., 1923)

THE MAKER OF NANTUCKET LIGHTSHIP BASKETS

"Did I read the price correctly on this?" the woman queries, feigning indifference. She has been browsing about at the crafts festival, encountering a range of prices and quality of workmanship, and quickly learning the deadpan response patterns of the seasoned shopper. Whether from shock or a keen desire to not be intimidated, she acquired the strategy of merely blinking, nodding, and smiling in response to the unexpectedly high prices she found on some items. Forty dollars for a pillow, seventy for a necklace—"Beautiful work," she would commend the artisans. This exhibit of Nantucket lightship baskets strains her new skills, though, and it is easy to see the disbelief in her raised eyebrows and hear the uneasiness in her voice. Three hundred dollars is simply a lot of money for a small, woven basket.

"You tell me what you read and I'll tell you if you read it correctly," the craftsman replies from the other side of the counter. As there is no mistaking the shock in the shopper's voice, there is no mistaking the indifference (some would call it disdain) in the artisan's. He slowly withdraws eye contact from her and focuses his attention on the thermos of lemonade he has been nursing all afternoon. His exhibit booth shades him from the powerful summer sun, and the breeze out of Hyannis helps to cool things off still more, but one gets the feeling that this man seldom heats up in any circumstances. Taking an occasional pull from his lemonade, he answers questions from some other shoppers and bids goodby to the woman (who departs, shaking her head).

He differs from most of the other craftsmen at the show—he is older, surer, more indifferent to customers. This indifference is actually the subject of some pride, as he attributes it to his Nantucket background. "If you come from Nantucket you're pretty damned independent to start with, and I guess I'm even worse than most of them." Where his Nantucket heritage left off in supplying him with old-style New England feistiness, his longevity and work in the craft took over. Williams Sevrens is, after all, the carrier of a genuine bit of Americana: the craft of making Nantucket lightship baskets.

Issues of price seem to crop up frequently in his talks

with customers. Many of them have real questions about the price, written carefully on the neat, white tag attached inconspicuously to the bottom of the baskets. Sevrens disposes of disparaging inquiries with real Nantucket style, but he's happy to discuss his work with anyone who is seriously interested. He explains that it usually takes forty hours for him to make a basket like the purse baskets on display. He starts with an oak log or plank and works it down to splits. "Imitators, they usually use split reed," he points out, "but for a snobby old Nantucketer you've got to have oak splits, staves, and hoops, and Java or Malay cane. We use green oak—you very seldom have to steam it if you get it green enough."

Mr. Sevrens takes considerable pride in the heritage of the lightship basket, tracing its history to "some bored guy on a lightship off Nantucket in the 1800s." A string of craftsmen in a Nantucket family carried on the craft over the years (Sevrens claims that it was banned by the Navy when its popularity got out of hand) until 1921, when Mr. Sevrens learned it from an ancestor of the original artisan. Sevrens was on vacation with his family at the time, and since he "hates the beach," he was happy to find a diversion.

Sevrens learned the craft slowly, starting by making parts of the basket and gradually learning how to put them together. Once he learned it, he still didn't have much of an idea that he might be able to make a living at it. He was a plumber, and the economic pressures of depressions and wars ruled out serious involvement with basket-making. He kept at it in his spare time, though, a little bit in the 1950s, then more in the 60s. "I wasn't thinking of doing it full-time," he recalls, "but then it just sort of happened." He knew he could make more money if he kept at plumbing but left because "I enjoy this much more."

Business is good for Mr. Sevrens despite (perhaps because of) his prices. Most of the people who look at the baskets on display don't buy them, but at his scale of operation he doesn't need a high volume. He casually points out to browsers that the baskets are not at all overpriced: "They're a bargain—last a lifetime. You can will them to your grandchildren." Even at his prices, he's got plenty of buyers. All fifteen of the display baskets were sold well before the show; he had to borrow them to have a display. "It's one of those things—you never seem to get ahead of yourself," he comments. Sevrens believes that he gets some customers because of his location on Nantucket (a bona fide Boston Brahmin vacation spot) and because of what he describes as a "radiation effect" among customers. His years of work on the island and extensive coverage by the media (he has been featured in all sorts of articles, including a piece in *The National Geographic*, back in the fifties) have helped make him an institution: "Now, I get calls from all over the country."

Success has brought some pressures: "I may well have got all the exposure I want," he worries. He looks on his current backlog of orders as a source of deadlines and schedules as well as of assured income. But success has also enabled Sevrens to expand a bit and take on several apprentices. A girl who had cleaned house for Sevrens and later, her boyfriend, asked him to teach them the craft. He agreed and developed a relationship that "feels like family now." The apprentices also help diversify the work, rotating different tasks to avoid boredom and providing some time for creativity and experimentation.

Mr. Sevrens long ago attained that state of development in crafts in which he could spend more time at his work itself than in worrying about whether he could do the work in an economically feasible way. His immediate prospects seem promising indeed and his personal needs seem to be met through his work. His longevity in the craft further underscores the reasonableness of his assumptions of continuing prosperity. His whole operation seems solid and permanent, yet he is as much subject to some pressures as beginning craftsmen struggling for survival.

Bill Sevrens is one of a growing number of people who make a full-time living in crafts work. His position within this number is notable for its stability and longevity and for his extreme devotion to the tradition of his craft. Like most craftspeople, he takes great pride in his work and relishes his independence.

Crafts has the potential to accommodate people like Bill Sevrens who value their independence and enjoy work in which they can pay serious attention to detail —to the details of the work in many respects as well as to the details of their personal lives. Increasingly, crafts are able not only to accommodate people like Sevrens, but also to provide them with the means to make a living.

Obviously not all craftspeople take their work as seriously as Sevrens or are as successful. In fact, the diversity of approaches within crafts make it interesting as a work arrangement: there are full-timers, many in more stable and lucrative situations than Sevrens, and part-timers who may only do one show each year; there are artists who disdain contact with customers, and artists who are mostly salespeople. The extreme flexibility of crafts renders difficult any accurate tally of who's doing what. At this point it is almost as difficult to accurately tabulate crafts organizations as crafts workers—the new breed of craftsfolk seems to be coming together in numbers and forms that make the older, lonely artists quake.

Meanwhile, the crafts scene itself has mushroomed to include fancy galleries, strict jurying of work for displays, and a plethora (some say it is approaching saturation) of exhibits and shows like the one in which Bill Sevrens participated. The national group, the American Crafts Council, famous for its yearly show in Rhinebeck, New York (people whose work gets accepted for it told me that the contacts they make there keep them busy all year), claims 37,000 members and puts out the monthly magazine *Crafts Horizons*.

Despite increasing formality, crafts is still an "occu- pation" marked by the ease with which people may and do enter it, and expand within it along paths they choose and design themselves. Crafts is a model of marginal work that underscores the seriousness of the genre and its flexibility and potential. At the same time, the experience of people in crafts vividly depicts the difficulties faced by people working on their own.

Crafts is notable for the ways in which it personalizes work. Writing about crafts, then, can best proceed with descriptions of people.

TWO TEXTILE ARTISANS

Linda and Geoff Post take turns staffing their display in the neat rows of crafts exhibits lining Boston's Pru- dential Center mall for a three-day autumn stint. A formidable stream of people flows through the mall but only a few seem even vaguely aware of the exhibits' encroachment on their normal business paths. They aren't "in a buying way." Those few who do stop at the Posts' display of pillows, hangings, quilts, and purses are the worst sort of customers: they ask ques- tions with perfectly obvious answers ("Did you make these yourself?") and they indiscriminately squeeze and massage the works on display. The Posts' response to questions and squeezes is an involuntary but heartfelt wince. To minimize the pain, only one of them minds the store while the other visits with other exhibitors, catching up on gossip, commiserating over the crowd, and addressing the universal question, "How's business?"

Despite the vagaries of the Prudential crowd, the Posts are still savoring their "conversion" to crafts. Until a few years ago, they had been teachers in a suburban New Jersey town. Teaching didn't quite meet their expectations, though, so they invested their savings and their growing knowledge of textiles in a move to a Western Massachusetts location. There, they rented a house large enough to provide work and display space and access to New England countryside and crafts markets.

They had participated in a few shows and worked at textiles for a bit in their spare time before the move, but their summary knowledge of both textiles and business management were almost embarrassingly minimal. Nonetheless, they were certain that they wanted to try. Geoff remarks, "There's just some point where you decide to throw all your time and money into it to make it work." At their point of decision the Posts confronted all the typical difficulties involved in any job switch and the insecurity of not knowing if they could make enough money to pay the bills. They had to buy additional supplies and acclimate themselves to a new life schedule as they made the switch from part- to full-time artisans.

They encountered basic problems in the day-to-day operations of their work, running out of materials they were sure they had in stock and money they were sure they had taken in. "Crafts is a funny thing unless

you've had the business experience," Linda explains.
They didn't have business experience and learned primarily through trial and error. The crafts environment
and the Posts' dedication to the idea helped them muddle
through in this way without starving, making learning
of the business aspects what Geoff calls "part of the
fun." With advice from friends, other craftsmen, and
a sympathetic accountant, they devised a straightforward bookkeeping system that enabled them to keep
track of orders, expenses and income.

Now, two years after the break from teaching, Geoff
observes, "Ends are starting to meet. We're paying
our bills. We're not eating pork and beans between
orders. We're down to working only twelve or fourteen
hours a day, seven days a week." Though the commitment and constraints seem extreme, Linda and Geoff
find them bearable and don't hesitate to express their
satisfaction with their work. "We're our own bosses,"
Geoff explains, "and you don't mind working for yourself. There's no one standing over you, you can do
what you want." In addition, they find that crafts work
meets their expectation of allowing them to spend more
time together. "Our relationship is much different
now," Geoff remarks. "We're together twenty-four hours
a day and we simply have to relate in ways that I never
even imagined before."

The Posts enjoy textiles but believe they could be
happy working at any of a number of crafts. "We don't
have a commitment to textiles per se," Linda notes,
"but to crafts in general." A good deal of the both
business and art experience they acquired in weaving
would stand them in good stead if they switched over
to leather or silver. They chose textiles initially because they had some experience in the field and because,
unlike such crafts as silversmithing or woodworking

that require expensive supplies or tools, a textiles "shop" could be started with minimal preparation and money. Also, they saw in the general area of textiles a lot of room for change and flexibility: textiles could be shaped into a variety of items in a wide range of work effort and end cost. Because they really didn't know so much about the craft, it made sense for them to be able to work at a diverse range of items to test the market and experiment with their own preferences.

Approaching their craft with this sort of objectivity, the Posts have developed a breadth of products (pillows, quilts, and purses were on display at their exhibit) and quality of workmanship. Geoff observes that it is getting increasingly important in crafts for work to be of high quality: "There's more craftsmen now, so there's more jurying for shows. We have to send in slides and pictures of our work and compete for space in shows that went begging for exhibitors a few years ago." In this growing culture, the Posts still manage to get into enough shows to sell enough to make a living. They experiment with new designs and new items and present a solid, attractive exhibit.

Geoff believes that the nature of their work has changed somewhat recently as they have been attending more wholesale shows. Galleries and boutiques send buyers to these shows to bring in a "line" of items, and craftsmen who sell to the buyers often contract for large numbers of stock items. "That's nice," Linda observes, "because it makes things much more efficient for us. We spend time on items we know will sell, and we don't have to hustle individual customers so much. The wholesale contracts take the life-or-death risk out of the whole operation. Of course, we're sacrificing some freedom because we have to produce a lot of the same item, and to their terms and contracts. But it gives us

a base. We can absorb a few bad shows, we can miss a
few individual sales. The contracts make it that much
easier to get by."

THE LANDSCAPE PAINTER

Expertly made up so that her reddened lips form the
perfect pout and her eyes register no expression whatever, the tall, rouged model is having a tough time trying
to give away the little samples in her wicker basket to
shoppers leaving Filene's. On other days shoppers
would move from the store to the great indoor corridor
of the Burlington (Massachusetts) Mall at a slow pace.
She could edge in, flash a smile, and disperse her material without much exertion. Today is more difficult,
though, because shoppers seem to be walking faster,
more purposefully. She has to walk fast, too, and that
is not very becoming to her demeanor, and physically
hard to manage in her skyscraper platform shoes. She
can still go after the slow ones, but mostly she simply
stands back and looks out into the corridor at the exhibit
of paintings that attract the shoppers.

In the middle of the broad corridor, beneath the high
skylight and next to the fountain lit with multicolors,
two racks of lucid New England landscapes exert the
pull over the shoppers. Featuring scenes of foggy
harbors, colorful mountains, and bleak snowfalls, and
mounted in rustic frames of weathered wood, the exhibit
commands a lot of attention. It is more successful at
turning heads than the frustrated model in Filene's
(who remains in rigid posture and expression, herself
staring across the corridor at the exhibit) and more
likely than most of the other 124 exhibits in the art show
to be remembered by shoppers. The landscapes' edge
over the model is a natural phenomenon, the result of

shoppers' interests, but the edge of the landscape exhibit over many of the others is more a matter of design and intentional planning. Chuck Selmi's reputation and collection of popular works ensure him a prime spot in the show, a location like the one at Filene's door, where he is assured of a good chunk of attention from the "best" groups in the mall crowd.

Shoppers probably give little thought to Selmi's location but other exhibitors can recognize it as a mark of status and success. With eight years experience, a solid collection, and a good sense of business, Selmi is well established. He owns a small gallery in North Conway, New Hampshire, and maintains a mailing list of 1,500 customers and friends. Several of the 125 people to whom he sent announcements of the Burlington Mall show came and chatted with him during our interview.

Selmi grew up in a business environment shaped primarily by his father, who was an automobile dealer. Following a brief stint selling Encyclopedia Britannica's Great Books, Selmi took up automobile sales. He was moderately successful, but unhappy. "If I had stayed, I would have gotten ulcers and become a grouchy old man," he recalls. "So at age 35, and with a wife and two children, I figured I should do whatever I was going to do quickly, so I could get established before I got too old. I had been exhibiting my art work in my spare time and I knew it would sell, so we took a gamble on it over the summer.

"It was a real gamble in the beginning, too. My wife had been happy with the security of the automobile business but unhappy with my being unhappy. She was understanding about the situation. Anyway, we made it through the summer all right. Then we had a very hard winter, but we stuck it out, and things got better." As soon as he could, he put his time and money in a gallery on Cape Cod, where he hoped the tourists would like and buy his work. He guessed the market right and tallied a substantial success in paintings of seascapes, sand dunes, and harbors. The work environment was taxing, though, as it required that he (and his family) keep the gallery open for long hours to meet the erratic schedules of tourists.

Selmi also found that the Cape Cod trade was interested almost exclusively in Cape paintings. "People expected seascapes, boats, dunes and that's pretty much all they wanted," he recalled. "I expected this somewhat, but not to that extent. I'm in this business to sell paintings and make a living, but I've got to feel good about what I'm doing, too. After two years at the Cape, we closed the gallery and moved to New Hampshire. That was great—it opened up a whole new world for me. I can travel for a few hours and paint Maine seacoast, Vermont countryside, or New Hampshire itself. New Hampshire tourists seem to be open to a broader range of paintings, too. I think they make a broader tour of New England than the people who visit the Cape."

Selmi credits his business background with providing much useful help in his art work. "I feel that the period I spent in the automobile business was invaluable," he claims. "There are some basic factors that apply to all business—some sense of market and price, and the whole idea of relating to a customer. So many of the artists that I see fall flat on their faces might have made it if they had any knowledge of management and accounting." It isn't that Selmi believes artists should be fast talkers or super salesmen. With his Encyclopedia Britannica sales background he knows people can be sold anything, but he won't "hard sell" his work and looks down on artists who do. "If the work won't sell itself, I won't peddle it." Besides, he's convinced that his soft-sell approach brings him more repeat customers.

Selmi believes that artists need to be less aware of their sales approach and more involved with an overall understanding of art as a form of business. This understanding includes respect for and knowledge of business issues, an ability to manage an uneven income flow and a sense of what constitutes a reasonable personal economic plan. When these issues clash with the concerns of art, Selmi contends that an artist should be pragmatic: "There are a lot of idealistic artists; very stubborn people interested in art only for its own sake. But to be a responsible family person, you've got to compromise somewhat." Selmi's pragmatism is not an absolute but a matter of degree, a balance between painting what he wants and what he knows will sell. When the tourist market at Cape Cod weighted the balance against his creative interests, he left. With his current gallery location in New Hampshire, Selmi can satisfy both the interests of his customers and the integrity of his art.

Though he is satisfied with the progress and quality of his art, Selmi shares with many other artists an annoyance with people who don't take him (and his work) seriously. "Some people will ask me the price of a painting—they're not interested in the painting, only the price. When I tell them how much it is, then they'll ask how long it took me. I tell them the truth—years of practice. I guess I really can't blame them. They come here to the mall and see me sitting here and reading, all relaxed and enjoying myself. They see the pictures all lined up on the rack, but they can't see all the work and the time I put into them. My old friends

in the auto business, they think I'm in semiretirement.
I do enjoy what I do, I love it, but I work very hard at it."

MUDFLAT

Outside, the building looks like any of the nearby light
industrial facilities in the neighborhood. It's several
stories high, constructed of now-dirty red brick, and
it looks oppressive, the sort of building intended to
house mind-numbing work and noisy machines, and
convey a generally dreary outlook on life. The Mudflat logo outside indicates that this is indeed the right
building. Inside, one follows posters up a flight of
steps, then through a narrow hallway past a bathroom
("Co-educational—please knock"). Reaching the
orange-juice machine, one is suddenly aware of a change
in the air quality. A fine haze of dust blurs normal
vision a bit and softens the glow of the ceiling lamps.
Everything is coated with the powdery stuff—lights,
shelves, doors, and of course, all the pots. Inexplic-
ably, the dust feels (and some say tastes) good. It's clay
dust, an inevitable by-product of the pottery craft, and
part of the atmosphere at Mudflat.

Like the aroma in a restaurant, clay in the air at Mudflat is only part of the overall experience. Where
restaurants provide tasteful visual settings and designs,
Mudflat displays clay in all sorts of forms (finished
pots, unglazed pots, broken pots, and indistinguishable
gobs of clay) to catch the eye. Where restaurants provide soft dinner music, Mudflat offers the industrious
rumble of the pottery wheels. Mudflat, a total experience in learning the pottery craft, offers a full course.

Mudflat is comprised of several rooms in the old
factory building, each one devoted to a particular
aspect of pottery. The first room one enters, to the

right of the hallway, houses ten motor-driven wheels and a shoulder-height brick kiln. When I visited, two people were shaping clay on the wheels, hunched over the spinning platters as if to scratch their noses with the evolving pots. Moving toward the back of the building, one passes through a small pantry containing powdered chemicals and colorants. The back room houses a cluster of kick wheels, a book rack, and a kiln the size of a small travel trailer. A sinister, powerful orange flame escapes up from the kiln into a ventilator. Over the entrance to the room of kick-wheel equipment, a carefully lettered poster warns: Do not, don't, you damn well had better not if you value your life, ever in the world get caught stepping on these flywheels with your full ungodly weight.

Many craftspeople incorporate educational activities into their normal operations as a way of keeping busy in slow times, improving their own techniques or experiencing the joy of involving new people in their craft. For a number of craftspeople, offering classes expands the interests and appreciations of customers and may become an important part of their work. Wholly devoted to teaching pottery, Mudflat is at an extreme end of the education continuum. Approximately five hundred people take courses at Mudflat each year, keeping its administrators/founders busy.

Ellen and Harvey Schorr started Mudflat with a friend, Bob Fenton, in 1971. Ellen and Bob were to have taught pottery for a local arts organization, but they suspected that the group was cheating artists and offering self-serving programs of poor quality. Since the group was not prepared to fund an adequate pottery program, Ellen and Bob decided to rent space and organize a pottery school on their own. The notion of working for themselves was exciting because it offered independence and a chance to run a high quality program. "One reason it was so appealing," Ellen recalls, "was that it allowed us to teach as well as we could possibly do it."

Ellen and the other teacher provided the artistic competence for the initial effort while Harvey supplied the more pragmatic inclination for business. "He certainly was the only one who knew anything about anything that had to do with business, or cared to learn. I knew half of nothing and Bob (the other teacher) knew less than nothing," Ellen acknowledges. The three committed themselves to several months of organizing, cleaning up, and investing salaries in costly equipment. High resale values reduced the risks involved; most every item could have been sold at a minimal loss if Mudflat didn't work out. After three months of investing all available money in capital equipment, they began paying themselves a living wage (between $125 and $150 per week). "What getting started really meant, more than anything else, was putting every cent the thing earned back into it," Ellen observes.

Mudflat attracted students and grew stronger in its first year, prompting the partners to incorporate and file for a charter as a nonprofit educational institution. Nonprofit status made Mudflat eligible to apply for grants, eliminated the necessity of paying unemployment and social security taxes, and was felt to be appropriate. (New laws require nonchurch, nonprofit groups to contribute to unemployment insurance.) Harvey explains, "A school should be nonprofit. A school shouldn't put money into anybody's pockets." At about the same time that the nonprofit status took effect ("The filing process took ages," Ellen recalls), Fenton left amicably "to go off to the woods and pot." The Schorrs stayed with Mudflat, developing it and making a living of their work.

Ellen experienced an unintended consequence of teaching pottery full-time. "I thought I would get to do more pottery," she observes, "but that hasn't been the case. One of my reasons for getting involved here in the first place was that I thought I would always have access to all the equipment. I'm usually too busy with administrative things to make any use of the equipment, though, and when I do have free time, I can't bring myself to look at it. I just get saturated."

Finding the interaction of teaching enjoyable, Ellen has worked rather extensively on teaching methods. In teaching advanced classes, she thinks less words make more learning: "I'm trying to say as little as possible. I show slides and try and get people working with the clay." In a typical throwing class, the reverse is true.

Although decisions are usually made with the involvement of the faculty, Ellen is recognized as the person who "knows the most about policy and the school." Most of the instruction is done by a few full-time staff members, though occasionally people are hired on a per course basis. There is also enough flexibility in Mudflat that everyone is and has to be committed. The organization also bends to meet student interests, offering rental time on equipment for people who want practice and free tuition for students who take on maintenance or support jobs. Although Harvey and Ellen have not consciously tried to establish a "sense of Mudflat," they believe "it's small enough so that people do have that sense."

Harvey's role at Mudflat is somewhat constrained by his lack of interest in the craft of pottery. "I've never really liked it," he remarks. "I don't like dirt. I have gotten into equipment ("He's a fine kiln builder," Ellen observes) but clay holds no fascination for me whatever." Harvey was trained as an architect at MIT and is registered to practice in Florida, but he is uncomfortable in the traditional modes of the profession. He has worked on housing research at the Harvard-MIT Joint Center of Urban Studies and taught architecture and been involved at the Boston Architectural Center. At Mudflat, he handles business matters and teaches kiln-building.

Harvey and Ellen agree that their work has not much affected their relationship. "There are times when I guess we see too much of each other," Ellen comments. "But I think that any problems we have are because we're in a lot of pressure situations, situations that create problems." Harvey observes, "I can be pressured in *any* situation, thank you."

Now in its fifth year, Mudflat reflects the downward slump of the economy in reduced enrolments, bottoming out at perhaps two-thirds of its level a few years ago. Ellen believes that people who now attend courses are "much more serious about pottery" than the students of earlier years. Noting that women (usually in the 21–26 age range) generally outnumber men in the classes by a ratio of about ten to one, she jokes that "We should run an adjunct dating service." Ellen has weathered cycles of enthusiasm and apathy over the past few years. "We'll be inactive for awhile, then, all of a sudden, there's a lot going on and it's exciting to be here again. It has to do with the students more than us. Also, every few years some new thing happens. New projects come along and get everyone's enthusiasm up." At the time of the interview, the new project under discussion was a branch of Mudflat to be set up in a barn in Maine. The branch would provide a live-in environment conducive to learning, an alternative to traditional apprenticeship arrangements, and a place to experiment with new technologies (like wood-burning kilns) not feasible in the city.

The Schorrs get as enthusiastic about the normal teaching work of Mudflat as they do about expansion plans. "Making a person into a potter is *very* difficult," Harvey points out. "Clay as a medium largely lacks constraints. It takes a long time to establish personal limits in a situation where anything is possible. Five years is a minimum for people to just gain technical competence, and after that, there's design." The complexity does not detract from, but enhances the lure of the craft, and Mudflat continues to convey the essence of the experience.

Bill Sevrens, the Posts, Chuck Selmi, and the Schorrs are all artisans earning a living from work that they make and sell as they choose. They share surface similarities: dependence on customers, some direct dealing with business and financial matters, some direct hands-on involvement with making something.

There are also surface differences: pricing policies, overhead, expectations and personal needs, ability, income. It's difficult to compare the overall situations of these artisans because there are so many factors to consider (some of which don't lend themselves to comparison) and because each situation is a system of interrelated parts. Bill Sevrens's approach to customers, his price policy and work schedule wouldn't make sense for Linda and Geoff Post. Furthermore, it would be difficult to alter any one aspect of any of the artisans' situations without altering and affecting other aspects. If Chuck Selmi were to try to sell his work in galleries instead of in shows, he would have to paint different subjects and establish a different way of thinking about customers.

Because different aspects of an artisan's work are so closely interrelated, it is often easy to predict much after seeing only a little. Seeing a craftsman's exhibit at a show, one may well be able to guess accurately at the nature of his work environment and his general approach to the craft. Part of this predictability follows from the ability of the craftsman himself to carry through into many aspects of the job some of the issues he feels are important, to integrate a general philosophy with a philosophy of work. While this integration embodies free expression across a broad range of issues often shut off to people working in large organizations, it may also limit the degree of variation possible within crafts work. Looking at Bill Sevrens, Chuck Selmi, and others who have found their niche, it is difficult to imagine them undertaking change or even serious consideration of change in any one aspect of their work. The interrelationship of aspects makes tinkering with any one of them a loaded enterprise.

To help articulate the range of available possibilities,

then, takes some disentangling from the personal systems described in the profiles in the earlier part of this chapter. In the cat's cradle of the personal systems each craftsman seems to set up, three large threads stand out: person, work, and sales. Exploring each of these should help to better approach the range of possibilities and the relationships between one and the others.

PERSONAL ISSUES

Personal issues, the beginning of work in crafts, incorporate personal histories, motivations, education, philosophy, and creative urges and help set the scene for the work and sales arrangements that people create. It is difficult to do justice to these issues in a written description because they may be very deep, very serious, and very emotional. These are the issues underlying the dramatic career switches one encounters in discussions with craftspeople who include former Ph.D.s and ex-convicts. These are the issues that traditional work arrangements could not satisfy, the basic issues that begin to explain "why" and bear the seeds of explaining "how."

One typical arrangement of personal issues is depicted by Chuck Selmi. His formal art education ended at his high school graduation, and his motivations to be a painter stemmed as much or more from wanting to get away from a pressured business environment (selling cars) as from wanting to paint. Like many others who turn to arts or crafts, he was pushed more than pulled. Unlike some others with whom I spoke, he was pushed mostly by the setting, not the content of his job. Selling cars as such didn't bother him so much as the pressure, the hustling, the environment that went with it.

(His prior job selling encyclopedias was unsatisfying in both content and setting.) Now with his painting, he makes a point of adopting a very low-key approach to customers and relies heavily on indirect contact by mail and repeat sales to satisfied buyers.

Randy McDaniel, a blacksmith from Frederick, Maryland, told me he was more dissatisfied with the content of his prior job. He was working on the design of bomb fuses as an engineering draftsman and quickly became bored and concerned with what he was doing. His dissatisfaction moved him to develop more intensively the blacksmithing skills he had been learning as a hobby. Similarly, Linda and Geoff Post began their work in textiles after finding that their teaching jobs did not meet their expectations. Seymour Friedman, a weaver from upstate New York, left a job in computer sales because of both the environment and content of the work. "I had had it with the business world," he remarked.

The possibility of independence in crafts work lures numerous people to the field as the limited existence of independence in traditional jobs helps push people out. Eleanor Dixwell Morrison, a quilter from Ashford, Connecticut, told me she wouldn't like to work for other people because it would mean "usually having to say yessir, nosir to someone else." She went on, "I like my independence. As long as I don't have to, why should I work for someone else?" Bill Sevrens put a lot of stock in independence in the content of his work and even in his sales, and virtually every artisan I've met has identified independence as part of the definition of his or her job.

Independence from "the boss" is easily, inherently attained in crafts work, but it sometimes brings with it problems of loneliness or isolation and may hinder attempts at intercraftspeople cooperation that could be beneficial. Also, the degree to which independence is tempered by dependence outside a crafts job (such as materials supply, shipping services, the sales market) can often run high and may severely hinder the independence of structuring one's own work. Despite these constraints on independence, which will be explored later in greater detail, it remains a powerful factor in crafts work.

Financial independence looms particularly large as one aspect of crafts that appeals to artisans. Concern for financial independence can take the form of dissatisfaction with other work expressed by the blacksmith Randy McDaniel: "I'm too ambitious to sit around in a place like that factory. You're stifled in there for what they let you do and the amount of money they let you make." Some craftsmen extend this view considerably, extolling the virtue of crafts as a system in which one may realize unlimited income potential. Bill Fontana, known as "Gepetto" to customers at his Hyannis toy shop of that name, frankly observes, "We're in it for the money. There's no limit to how much you can make." Linda and Geoff Post partially express this view, with Geoff noting, "One reason for doing this is that I can be my own boss, that we can go as far as we want." All this is not to say that craftspeople are a money-hungry lot but to point out that the financial lure of crafts is often part of crafts work. For some reason, many people unfamiliar with crafts work associate it with dabbling dilettantism; this simply is not the case, especially for people who work at their crafts as a way to earn a living. Though it seldom seems to become an obsession, the financial potential of crafts is always some part of the picture.

The total crafts work situation is also a lure for some people who are attracted by the combination of factors involved. Eleanor Dixwell Morrison views this combination as "a challenge," a personal issue, and a different way of thinking about work. In establishing Mudflat, Ellen Schorr viewed the combination as a chance to "do something as well as it could possibly be done." Numerous craftspeople pointed out that the appeal of crafts was in its flexibility, its allowing one to make of it whatever one chose.

For people attracted to this combined lure, the craft itself may not be important. Like Linda and Geoff Post, they may talk casually of switching. Their entry into crafts may be like that of Stephen and Christina Strait (a pewtersmith and weaver, respectively, of Middletown, Connecticut), who researched books on crafts to find appealing materials and products. This may seem like a lighthearted Sears catalog sort of endeavor, but is really much more serious. Stephen Strait made a dramatic career switch, leaving behind his research and master's degree in applied physics. He views the switch as an inevitability, something that simply had to be done, and looks on his education as time not wasted but well spent as it "affects the way I look at the world."

Some craftspeople are not converts from computer sales or applied physics but people who have grown up with and been socialized into crafts as a way of life. Their motivations may encompass the desire for independence and control expressed by converts, but they are usually more concerned about the craft as such. Their training may have begun in their families at an early age or in formal arts and crafts programs in technical schools and colleges. For those people thoughts of a casual switch in crafts would approximate blasphemy. Basket weaver Bill Sevrens is one example of such a craftsman, someone who is involved more in doing the craft than the environment that goes along with it.

To some extent, some of this identification with one's craft is inherent—after all, the work is a matter of choice and people choose what suits them. The labels "leather person," "weaver," "blacksmith" thus strike a more personal note than "account clerk." The toymaker in Hyannis assured me "I *am* Gepetto." People who have a long, deep background in their craft may well approach sales as a necessary evil that helps them pay the bills while they continue their quest for the ultimate wall hanging, pottery planter, or patchwork quilt.

Craftspeople who have far-reaching backgrounds in their craft seem less likely to approach their work with the rhetoric of "alternatives" that seems endemic to converts. After several years of arts college and perhaps another few years of apprenticeship or individual study, a craftsman can justifiably look on his work as a career. He has few of the feelings of lucky escape mentioned by converts who may experience some difficulty in coming to terms with the seriousness of the work. Theoretically, it would be possible for a craftsman with much training and experience in a craft to become obsessively involved in the pursuit of the craft and recreate within the craft aspects of a work environment like those in traditional business.

In fact, there seem to be very few such people, and their numbers seem limited by the crafts "market" and by the human limits of involvement. The crafts market enables people to gain followings and reputations that can support more limited production and a greater concentration on design. In other words, people with more experience can produce less but think more about what they do. This seems true for both "stayers" born and raised (and/or educated) in a craft and for "switchers" from another type of career. Stayers, however, are often further along in this process than switchers of

similar ages, simply because they've been at it longer.
This characteristic path to more design and less production reduces the pressure on experienced craftsmen
and helps them maintain a reasonable level of involvement with their work. The crafts market allows them
to devote more time to the more intellectually interesting
problems of design, making the work more interesting
as time goes on. The market thus directs people away
from obsession with production. Conversely, the
psychological limits of saturation (depicted well by
Ellen Schorr at Mudflat) also restrict obsession in
production. People burn out, get tired, bored, lazy,
or interested in something else.

Both stayers and switchers seem to respond to the
flexible aspect of work in crafts that allows, even encourages them to change. Work in arts or in a craft
is often defined as a developmental process, with considerable emphasis placed on change over time. Craftspeople tell the story of their improvements and changes
in design as though describing the growth of a gifted,
cherished child. In addition, the rhetoric (though not
always the actuality) of fields of artistic expression
is that they reward creativity, new ideas, unorthodox
techniques. This rhetoric stands in often dramatic
opposition to the situations that people encounter in
traditional jobs and helps supply a continuing incentive
for people to remain and grow in arts and crafts.

A final, seldom-mentioned, but necessary personal
element in crafts work is failure or incompetence at
traditional work that usually does not figure in artisans'
autobiographical accounts of their work. Failure is
a part of the traditional environment, though, and its
prospect may help a craftsman formulate a "You can't
fire me—I quit" mentality that concentrates on the potential of the craft he is coming to rather than the failure

situation he is leaving. Even though this is the case for many switchers, it does not detract from the nature of crafts as an alternative but stresses the value of crafts in encompassing a diverse set of needs and criteria for success.

Even if this is the case for many switchers, it does not detract from the nature of crafts as an alternative but stresses the value of crafts in encompassing a diverse set of needs and criteria for success though the situation is changing somewhat. Crafts are still relatively free of entry barriers and credentialing mechanisms like degrees and diplomas. What counts most is not what craftspeople have but what they *produce*.

From this very mixed array of personal concerns, craftspeople approach their daily working and selling situations. One may correctly suppose that the diverse range of personal concerns lays a foundation for diversity in working and selling arrangements.

WORK

Randy McDaniel is no Charles Atlas. Those are real muscles on his arms all right, but he just doesn't possess the overall bulk one normally associates with blacksmiths. He's decked out with a leather apron over his T-shirt, leaning carefully over the charcoal fire. He holds the metal form-in-process in a forceps in his left hand and hammers down firmly with his right. There's a resounding clink and one can see, unmistakably, a visible change in the metal. Another clink, another change. More clinks, and the metal changes in a continuum like slowly passing frames of a motion picture or action under a strobe light. Randy, now dripping with perspiration from exertion and the heat of the fire, stops to add some coal. Working the bellows, he fans the flames, sending clouds of smoke and soot into the air.

Coughing, bystanders surrounding his exhibit at the crafts festival step back but continue watching. As the wind changes direction, the shape of the crowd also changes to allow the smoke to escape without asphyxiating them. They are all accumulating a thin layer of fine black dust on their faces and clothes, but nothing to compare with the gunk building up on Randy, who is beginning to look like a coal miner in a sauna. As the metal is unmistakably changing under the influence of Randy's hammer, his expression is unmistakably stable.

Blacksmithing work is colorful in the extreme; few other types of arts and crafts work can match it for sheer theatrical quality. Even people at the outermost fringes of Randy's exhibit can easily get some feeling for what is going on. Randy confirms the enthusiasm he projects: "I would like to do this for the rest of my life. Not just the work, but the lore and the history of it keep you involved." It's easy to see him leaving behind his work as an engineering draftsman on the bomb fuse project—the clean office, the rows of well-lit drafting tables, the work itself. In terms of simple appeal, there is no comparison between the two jobs. Gepetto the toymaker enjoys a similar kind of obvious work appeal. He notes, "This is fun. I like dealing with children. I can work and have a good time at it, be like a kid myself."

Beyond appeal, the commonalities between Randy McDaniel's work and other crafts become more obvious. At a crafts show, one can often observe blacksmiths, weavers, potters, carpenters, toymakers, quilters, and a host of others at work. Organizers of exhibits encourage craftsmen to have displays that include production set-ups because they know that the set-ups are certain crowd-pleasers. While observing all these artisans in one place, one is struck first by the diversity of work spaces that they created. Within the small exhibit spaces, each artisan somehow manages to create a custom environment that is unique among the lot. One can readily imagine a carry-through of the environments on display at the show to the artisans' full-time workshops and studios. Second, one is struck by the similarity of the intensity projected by all the artisans engaged in work. Without the fire and brimstone, Randy McDaniel looks basically the same as the working weavers, potters, toymakers and carpenters: terribly involved.

Full-time work environments set up by craftspeople and artists further mirror the range of individual tastes. Some of the diversity in the look of workspaces follows from the crafts themselves, as each craft has its own retinue of tools, work settings and by-products. A silversmith's shop has to differ from a carpentry shop, for example, because it lacks saws, wood tools, and sawdust. Within the inherent limits imposed by the crafts, it would be possible for a craftsperson to set up a work environment that reflected little concern for the craft itself. In carpentry, for example, saws can be quieted and floors vacuumed regularly. In silver-smithing, tools could be left sitting on counters and clutter could be allowed to accumulate.

It appears, however, that the work of a craft is a powerful predictor of the way the shop environment will look: carpentry shops sport sawdust layers on everything (as Mudflat had its clay dust) and silver-smith shops tend to look like they've been cleaned and straightened by the same meticulous hands that shape the silver. The craft itself, then, sets the basic material environment in its mandatory link to particular tools and supplies. In addition, the art or craft seems influential in setting the tone of the work. While a weaver and a blacksmith may both approach their work with a great deal of intensity, the weaver can't "go" at his craft with the same tone as the blacksmith. Each has its own tone, its own pace underlying the work. Craftspeople can (and do) alter the pace and tone of their work, but the work supplies part of the pace itself, a basic part with which a craftsperson must contend.

Some craftsmen contend with the pace of their work by thoroughly immersing themselves in it, producing at high volume during long, unbroken work days. By all accounts, a twelve-hour work day is not uncommon, and the claim of Linda and Geoff Post to have finally gotten *down* to a twelve-hour work day (from fourteen) raises eyebrows only among those unacquainted with crafts. With their lack of experience, expertise, and reputation, beginners in an art or craft must work harder and longer than more seasoned artisans, but experience is in itself no guarantee of success. Increasing numbers of people are making a living in arts and crafts, but not without considerable effort. Beginners can look forward to some alteration in their work to incorporate more interesting tasks, but the prospects for leisure are not good. Vacations and time off cost an artisan money, and no paycheck comes in when an artisan is idle. Some craftspeople manage to attain a comfortable work pace and earn a comfortable living, a few even get wealthy; but the norm seems to be an extension of the tortoise's dictum: slow and steady, persistent, exhaustive, unrelenting.

All craftspeople and artists balance the external pressures for production and survival through flexibility and adaptation not possible in traditional work arrangements. Because their work is "closer to home," artists and craftspeople can more closely match control of their work environment to personal needs. If a holiday or important purchase is coming up, they can intensify their efforts to meet their needs. They can also make such an adjustment on a long-term basis, defining a "comfortable living" within a broad range and setting their levels of effort and production accordingly. Beyond this general flexibility, craftspeople can hedge against oppressive work loads and survival by changing the structure of their work hourly, daily, weekly, or monthly, switching from one aspect of their work to another. Numerous artisans alternate among work on small, medium, and large items, and throw in some work on bookkeeping, records, setting up exhibits, and "doing a show" for the sake of variety.

These "secondary tasks" tend to be overlooked in a craftsperson's definition of his work, but they can be quite time-consuming and crucial to survival. The whole system aspect of crafts work makes it more interesting, provides more ground in which a craftsperson can exert influence and control. This can distract the purist interested only in production and design and can be handled for these people in a desultory way. For nonpurists, part of the lure of arts and crafts work is in its potential for input not only in design and production, but in sales, marketing, and distribution as well.

One way a craftsperson can alter the pace of his work is to break it down, to approach it as a small assembly line. The quilter (pillows, quilts, notebooks) Eleanor Morrison cuts material and lays out pieces in sets of sixes and twelves. "You can do things in half the time, when you work with six," she observes. "You go from one medium to another—cutting, laying out, sewing. In a small way, I mass produce. I'm a great enthusiast for the time studies." This sort of breakdown of work is possible in lots of crafts: carpenters can work on one part of a cabinet; toymakers on one wheel of a truck. Some painters do ten pictures at once by painting one color and one area at a time in each.

Even when the work does not lend itself to segmenting (blacksmithing must be done continuously on the anvil as weaving is done on a loom), it is possible to set up a variation on segmentation by producing "stock items," objects that require relatively little work and sell for relatively little money. Ms. Morrison's quilt-covered notebooks are stock items, as are Randy McDaniel's dinner bells. Craftspeople produce stock items in response to the mixed motives of wanting to work at a range of scales and wanting to have something to sell to browsers at shows and exhibits uninterested in more serious pieces. However, even when craftsmen produce numerous stock items, they appear concerned about the originality and quality of their work. Several pointed out to me the advantages of the stock item of their design over other similar items in a show.

A craftsperson's decision of how to structure his work depends on what and where he thinks he can sell. If he is inexperienced and without a following or reputation, he may feel compelled to sell his wares only in shows or exhibits at which low prices are the order of the day; he may produce mostly or only stock items. If he is dealing with items that have low prices and is trying to make a living from his work, he will have to sell a lot to get by and will have to produce a lot to keep up. A craftsperson's perception of what will sell and at what price, then, operates as one parameter of his production process. His liking of a particular kind of production or of a particular balance of different kinds of production is another.

Eleanor Morrison keeps busy doing custom work, but

she continues making things to sell in shows "for entertainment and relaxation." Geoff and Linda Post aspire to a high enough level of wholesale business to give them a subsistence income. Dealing with wholesalers means having to produce very intensively, but that does not seem to be a problem for them. Pewtersmith Stephen Strait is moving away from high levels of production toward more design. He is more interested in working on "things that you might be remembered for. . . . If the day comes when I feel like I'm just doing production, it'll be time to move on."

A recurring controversy crops up in crafts around the issue of mixing work space and selling space. Bill Sevrens thinks a shop would drain his time and money: "Once you have a shop, your overhead goes way up. I don't think it's worth it. You have rent, advertising." Stephen Strait notes, "It seems to me that being a craftsman and being a shopkeeper are two different things. The shop is a hassle to run—it takes long hours and rents are expensive. It's difficult to get work done. People think you're available to talk any time. We once had a whole Brownie troop come in, unannounced, and practically ask us to perform so they could see us at work. I'd like to see them do that in an insurance company, to just walk in and say, 'Show us how you fill in forms.'"

Strait does feel, however, that the shop was useful when he and his wife were just starting their business. It gave them a place to be, and the combination of pewtersmithing and weaving created a pleasant atmosphere and an interesting range of products. The shop helped them focus on the work and, despite high costs, always managed to pay for its own expenses. Even Bill Sevrens agrees that a shop is right for some people: particularly, he thinks, for those who work with mass-produced crafts.

SALES AND SHOW BUSINESS

When Jinx Harris says, "It's me, I am the boss," one's
thoughts turn to similar statements made by others:
"I am the President," "L'Etat c'est moi." Ms. Harris
probably wields as much power in her realm of activity
as the sources of the other two quotes did in theirs,
but she manages to do it with style, grace, and the
respect of the people she's "bossing." Jinx Harris is
(as the movie ads might put it) Jinx Harris Productions,
the promoter and organizer of some forty-four professional art, crafts, and sculpture shows held each year
in suburban shopping malls on the East Coast. Nearly
2,600 artisans apply to Ms. Harris for space. In deciding who may exhibit, she exerts a major source of control over what sorts of arts and crafts a large public
will be exposed to.

As she prepares, clipboard in hand, to take the morning attendance roll call at the mall show, she informs
me that, "Now's my time to be bitchy." Her show rules
demand that every exhibitor be on hand at the mall
early for each morning of the show, a rule that many
late-rising artisans find troublesome. Even those who
normally are early risers get worn out by the second
or third day of a show after putting in twelve-hour days
on the mall floor. She has her standards, though, and
anyone watching her embark on her morning inspection
tour could tell from the speed and force of her walk
that she means business. I struggle to keep up with
her, hoping for the artisans' sake that they are all in
positions at their assigned places in the mall's airy
central boulevard.

Nestled there amid fountains, benches, and large
potted plants, the exhibitors (all 130 of whom were
present and accounted for) look up and smile as Jinx
walks by, the more familiar ones calling out a greeting

or asking a quick question. No greetings or questions
break her pace, though, and as she finishes the tour
and we head for one of the mall's coffee shops it is
obvious that her claim to being the boss is accurate
and perhaps even modest. For a brief moment when
the coffee shop staff greet her and a waitress proceeds
unasked to pour and mix her tea, it appears that Ms.
Harris's reign might extend to the coffee shop. However, it was familiarity and not authority made her
known in the shop. Watching her unfold her papers,
it becomes apparent that the coffee shop is one of a
series of itinerant offices that she appropriates during
her travels.

The craftspeoples' greetings gave the lie to Jinx's
intention of being bitchy. They were obviously pleased
to see her, however much they may have been inconvenienced. Several of them later remarked that they
respected Jinx's hard-nosed approach to exhibitions
because it made for better shows and more sales. She
herself provided some detail of her approach to exhibitions in a sample of the applications she has exhibitors
fill out (page 65) for her shows.

At first glance, these rules may seem petty, irrelevant
and oppressive. However, craftspeople respond to the
rules as serious business and remark on how Ms.
Harris's shows always present a good appearance.
"You can always tell a Jinx Harris show," one weaver
told me. "All the exhibits look good, and the show
is pleasant and enjoyable to walk through." A painter
told me that the rules were all in support of the artists,
aimed at improving everyone's business, and that Jinx
was a strong debunker of "Mickey Mouse requirements"
like dress codes for exhibitors that some mall manage-
ments attempted to enact. The painter noted his belief
that Jinx is "all for the artist." He remarked that he

Jinx Harris Shows, Inc.

R.F.D.#1 BOX 153J
AUBURN, NEW HAMPSHIRE 03032
(603) 483-2742

Dear Exhibitor:

1. SHOWS START ON DIFFERENT DAYS — CHECK CAREFULLY — YOU WILL NOT be allowed to set up a day late because you did not read the application.

2. NO LIGHTS, except battery operated permitted. Only exception . . . equipment used by craftsmen and lights for sketch artists - batteries must be in a plastic or wooden box.

3. No toddlers, children or pets at any show. Please make arrangements to leave them AT HOME.

4. A space is one (1) rack or one (1) table . . . two portfolios only per space. NO EXTRA TABLES, ETC. WILL BE PERMITTED — having too much in your space makes a messy show and isn't fair to your fellow exhibitor.

5. All exhibitors must have exhibits completely up by 10 A.M. opening day — NO EXCEPTIONS. All exhibits must remain open until word is given that the show has ended. Anyone tearing down early at any show will not be allowed in any future shows — NO EXCEPTIONS. This also means that no dollies or any other packing material be brought into the mall until word has been given that the show is over.

6. PARKING of ALL exhibitors vehicles must be far away from the mall as possible at all times — give the customers the parking areas near the mall.

7. All tables must be covered on all four sides to the floor — not with white sheets. All supplies must be out of sight at all times.

8. No picnicing on the mall at any time.

9. You must make sure that your area is SPOTLESS when you leave the mall — anyone found leaving a messy area will be denied entrance into future shows.

10. NO CONFIRMATIONS are sent — your check is your receipt. Applications and checks will be returned to you if the show is filled. If you reserve a space in a show — you are responsible for paying for that space. NO REFUNDS for any reason after closing date!

11. All problems should be taken up with the Director of the show — NO EXHIBITOR may go to the Mall Manager, Security, Janitors, Electricians or Merchants.

12. Unprofessional conduct, inappropriate dress, and not manning your exhibit are due cause by Directors for removal from mailing list or show.

13. NO RACK may exceed 6' 6'' — no exceptions.

14. No placing of chairs, or anything in front of stores — at any time!

15. NOTE PAPER may not be sold unless the original is on display.

16. Leather craftsmen — Absolutely not more than ten (10) buckles to be exhibited without belts. You are leather craftsmen NOT BUCKLE SALESMEN — NO BUCKLES SOLD SEPARATELY.

17. IF YOU USE A TORCH, the flame area must have an 18'' (min.) shield on three sides. You must also have a fire extinguisher and a protective tarp, or equivalent, on the floor.

felt much better about entrusting the sales of his work to someone who was as conscientious about the selling as he was about the work itself. Along these lines, Ms. Harris points out that she is one of the only promoters who "stays on twelve hours a day" during a show to provide moral and material support where needed.

This Burlington (Massachusetts) Mall show is an all-arts show, one of ten Ms. Harris organized for the 1975-76 season. She also promoted seventeen crafts-sculpture shows and fifteen crafts-only shows. All the shows were popular, but Ms. Harris believes the crafts shows are currently the most popular. She recalls, "Eight years ago, I couldn't even get a crafts show together. I had to offer prizes, trips to Europe, in order to lure enough artisans to make up a show. The story is much different now, of course. There's a general interest among shoppers in crafts now and there are many more artisans. In the malls, people like the crafts shows because they can usually afford to buy some of the items. The arts and sculpture shows are nice, but the paintings and sculpture are often fairly expensive."

Ms. Harris's forty-two mall shows are placed in large, mostly suburban shopping malls, locations she terms "the best malls on the East Coast." One might wonder why such malls would want to rent their prime corridor space to anything, much less a show that might compete with its own tenants. "They do it because every [mall], no matter how successful, needs promotion," Ms. Harris claims. "The shows bring out people who normally would be sitting at home, and everyone at the mall benefits. As far as the competition, there are usually a few stores whose business does compete with the show. They either get outvoted by the others or they ride with the majority and ask for restrictions on the sale of specific items. A few malls simply don't allow leather or jewelry crafts. Also, I never book a show during Thanksgiving, Christmas, Mother's Day. . . . The merchants would scream and holler."

The mall as an institution offers a unique forum for arts and crafts shows, exposing people who might not otherwise come into contact with crafts to the wares and people of the arts and crafts culture. Jinx Harris characterized malls as a kind of people's art gallery: "This is where John Q. Public sees his art, not in galleries. The mall has taken over the place of the corner drug store. It's always amazing to me that the malls are crowded on Saturday nights—whole families out strolling around. The mall is an entertainment center, and it doesn't cost anything."

Recognizing the potential conflict between what mall audiences are used to and what artists produce, Ms. Harris established, early on, baseline personal standards for her shows. She stresses that her shows are not to be called "arts and crafts" shows because "that means little old ladies with jams and jellies." The shows are "Professional Art Festivals," including crafts, or "Professional Craft and Sculpture Shows."

More important to her than the names of the shows are what's in them. She has "a personal vendetta against plastic and paper flowers." She also isn't keen on paintings on velvet (99 percent of which come from Mexico, she claims), plastic jewelry, and anything that is "commercial looking." This still leaves a broad range of activities from which she must choose, and while she realizes that the growing ranks of crafts people have raised the quality of the shows, she agonizes about the difficulties of choosing.

Beyond the decisions of putting together balanced

shows (of a diversity of arts and crafts) that will please mall crowds, she also must figure in the knowledge that people are (or aren't) making a living based on her decisions. In the last round of applications, she reviewed color slides of work, categorizing of crafts by type and show, matching exhibitors with floor plans of the shopping malls, and trying to follow a principle of including each applicant in at least one show. She also bases some of the decision on artisans' track record in previous shows, reflecting not only on their work, but on their personality as well. "If they're chronic complainers, I don't need them," she remarks. She sees no way of making the process completely objective and knows that no matter how careful she is, she will make some wrong choices. Rejecting anyone for any reason pains her, and she points out that, "At the end of the selection process, I feel like a heel."

Craftspersons and artists who have been selected for shows receive notification months in advance so they can plan their circuits. They pay an average of thirty dollars, a flat fee for their spaces in a show. Ms. Harris uses flat fees rather than taking a commission on sales as some promoters do because "then I'd have two thousand enemies instead of two thousand friends." She believes the flat fee system also makes more business sense because it requires less bookkeeping.

After paying their fee and receiving confirmation of their acceptance for a show, artisans usually won't have any contact with Jinx Harris Productions until the day of or before the show when, according to Jinx, "surprisingly few" problems or absences occur. At one time, navigational difficulties caused some absences—people who came from out of state had trouble finding the malls. This has been partially remedied by the distribution of a "Jinx Harris Productions" bumpersticker to exhibitors and the increasing popularity of citizens' band radios. Ms. Harris describes traveling to a show as a "caravan" and notes that exhibitors frequently stop to help "brothers" having problems on the road.

In a way, Ms. Harris's organizing of a show resembles the work of the artists and artisans. She crafts a show as an event as much as Linda and Geoff Post do a quilt or Randy McDaniel a candelabra. She takes care of her material and is extremely conscientious about the finished product. Like the artisans, she looks on the work as a learning process: "Each time, I get a little sharper—and a little bitchier." Like many craftspeople, she traces her work back to "an idea"—in her case, the notion, about ten years ago, that her home town of Atlantic City could improve summer boardwalk business by running an art show. Also, like many craftspeople, she took the initiative—to convince the town that the show could be done, that she could do it, and finally, surprising herself: "I didn't know from nothing. I would make phone calls, send out mail, assign spaces, and all of a sudden—there was an art show."

Following those early shows came her growing realization of the need of artists for winter exhibits if they had realistic plans of making a full-time living from their work and matching that realization with a visit to what appeared to be the perfect spot for an exhibit —the then-new Cherry Hill Mall in central New Jersey. She approached the mall management, ran the show well, and discovered that such events have a way of becoming annual repeats. She began to approach more malls (some approached her), and she built the show into an operation, a full-time job for herself and eventually also for her husband who handles finances and accounting. Now even one of her teenage sons, Tom, is involved as a full employee with full power. Unfortunately, most of the work is in traveling, staying in motels, and time spent in the malls themselves.

Jinx points out that while the malls may supply environments conducive to buying, they are not the best for working. The canned air has a way of making one feel lightheaded after a few hours and the canned music sets an unnaturally jaunty cadence. "And those fountains they put in the corridors," Jinx observes, "have a definite effect on making you go to the bathroom. I never can set up shop near them myself, and I have to be real careful about setting up exhibitors near them—they won't talk to me after spending a show running to the bathroom."

Jinx Harris's mall shows are certainly not the only medium through which artisans can sell their work, but they are representative of "the exhibit" mode that puts artisans in touch with potential customers. The mall shows are noteworthy because, unlike most crafts fairs, they are held in an environment that features a captive, guaranteed audience. The issue at most fairs is not competition with established merchants but attendance at the fair. Malls have a sort of guaranteed minimum level of activity regardless of the presence of a show, but the activity may produce only minimal sales. At a show (also organized by Jinx Harris) held at Boston's Prudential Mall, I sat with artisans and watched the lunchtime crowds ebbing and flowing through the exhibits, but never really stopping to look and buy. Audiences at a crafts show may be fewer in number, but people are usually more interested in the show. At mall shows, people may be uninterested in the crafts and hostile to the whole arrangement.

In any kind of show, artists and artisans are placed

in the position of having to sell their own work directly, face-to-face, to customers. One painter at the Burlington Mall show described such sales as "a real ego trip." People ask, 'Did *you* really paint it?' They tell you how much they like your work and actually pay you for it right there. You get to experience the full cycle of your work. You're like an actor on a stage." Not all artists enjoy the salesman role, though, and some find that it conflicts completely with their interests and their style. Chuck Selmi's approach of allowing the work to sell itself is a compromise many seem to have reached.

Outdoor shows seem to be flourishing in the summer, and many are managed very well. Some, however, are run by inexperienced groups ["Every town's Chamber of Commerce wants to be in on the act," Jinx Harris observes] and most are at the mercy of the weather. Gepetto the toymaker told me about a promoter who charged very high rents but did not come through with the publicity he promised. The show was a failure, drawing few customers to the exhibitors who had traveled miles to put their work on display. The artisans wasted their time and didn't even have any recourse to make the promoter accountable.

Even when shows are well organized, competently promoted, and extensively advertised there is no guarantee that they will be well attended or profitable. The first Cape Cod Artisans Revival, held in the summer of 1975 at a prime Cape location, was a good show that attracted less activity and attendance than its extensive advertising and public relations campaign should have drawn. Dispirited artisans could be heard in the afternoon calm, addressing the blue sky with questions regarding the whereabouts of all the legendary Cape Cod vacationers. Some exhibitors, like Bill Sevrens,

thought the promoters had missed their bet by sticking
with traditional approaches to promoting the show.
"They did their advertising by the book," he remarked,
"and the book wasn't written for the Cape." He thought
the promoters would have done better to have gotten
some mention in the *New York Times* travel section
than to have concentrated on traditional advertising.
Other exhibitors had similar Monday morning quarter-
backing analyses of the show's problems. No one,
however, really blamed the promoters, and the exhibitors at the Cape show voiced an opinion that I heard
echoed at every show by every exhibitor: "It's always
a gamble."

A number of artists view sales with considerably
less fervor, regarding it as a necessary evil with which
they put up to pursue their craft or perhaps seeing it
as a demeaning chore best left to others more suited
to it. The psychological rewards of selling one's own
work also have a nasty flip side, with the potential for
stripping at least as great as the possibilities for ego
tripping. A confident artisan can hold his or her own,
but an inexperienced, unsure, or unstable (as artists,
after all, have a reputation of being) artisan can be
devastated by the offhand remark of a casual browser.
Some artisans, like Bill Sevrens, protect themselves from
this problem by developing a hard-nosed approach to
all customers, while others, like Chuck Selmi, make a
point of being low-key.

Customers' generally low level of understanding of
crafts seems to help strengthen an artisan's psychological stance—it is usually obvious that people who
ask potentially threatening questions simply don't know
any better. Gepetto the toymaker told me how, when
a woman insisted that the items for sale in his shop
were not made by him but imported from Japan, he

refrained from arguing because he knew he wouldn't convince her of anything. A weaver at the Prudential Mall show told me, "Everyone who stops to ask you about your work thinks he's the first one to ask you anything. Some of them have a chip on their shoulder, like they're out to prove that you're a fraud, but most of them just don't know."

A recent issue of *Sunshine Artists*, a magazine published for artisans and artists featured a list of remarks overheard at art fairs that helps articulate what exhibitors encounter. Some classics from the list:

How long did it take you to do this?
How much is it without the frame?
This is nice stuff. What do you do for a living?
Has anyone ever told you that you paint just like Andrew Wyeth?
"I'm going to buy that, Hazel, it's absolutely gorgeous!"
    "Don't bother, Muriel, I'll make you one just like it."
Don't you have something a little smaller in red?[1]

GARDEN STUDIO

Emily Huntley offers another way of selling arts and crafts for artisans who don't enjoy the show scene or want to supplement their income from it. Ms. Huntley runs a small, comfortable gallery in a modest, cozy, single-family home a block off a main street in Greensboro, North Carolina. Her approach is like that of Jinx Harris, but turned upside down and inside out. Her operation is based on a stationary location, repeat customers, and a relatively slow pace.

Ms. Huntley calls her gallery "Garden Studio." It boasts a large yard occasionally given over to the display of outdoor sculptures, and a porch that begs to be used for some moments of conversation and contemplation of the birds singing in the surrounding trees. Inside, custom furniture, sculpture, pottery, and paintings tastefully fill the house. There is also some workspace for Ms. Huntley, herself an artist, and a small apartment upstairs where her son lives.

Emily Huntley got into the gallery business after years of teaching painting and drawing at a local college. She originally started the place as a co-op with much moral support from a small group of friends. The idea came up at a group lunch, and she went ahead and developed it. The group still lunches weekly, a "hilarious, two-hour lunch that you could hear up to the street-corner," Ms. Huntley thinks. The group provides lots of ideas, support, and fun.

Garden Studio is fairly busy, considering that the only advertising it uses is a small spot in the local press. There are other ways of getting the word out, though, and the local media have been generous with newspaper story space and TV time covering various exhibitions and the gallery itself. The dirt road leading down from the main street carries a comfortably substantial number of people to Garden Studio, people attracted primarily by the most effective advertising of all: word of mouth.

Ms. Huntley draws between one and two hundred names from her master list of five hundred in publicizing the opening of a new show, an event that occurs about ten times yearly. About two hundred people usually come to the openings, and then every day for weeks after the crowds continue so that usually she is never alone in the house. Ms. Huntley feels that unlike some shows, her gallery is not at all affected by bad weather—the crowds keep coming. It is easy to see why—anyone who has been to Garden Studio would see its potential as an especially cozy place on a rainy day.

The mailing list and Ms. Huntley's informal connections and networks of friends and colleagues are the studio's mainstay. There are no memberships or sponsors. She charges exhibiting artists a yearly fee of ten dollars and takes 25 percent of any sale. She doesn't attempt to influence an artisan's prices in any way, and she says she is a bit of a pushover for exhibitors. She finds it difficult to turn an exhibitor away if she doesn't think his or her work is up to par.

Garden Studio provides a service Ms. Huntley believes is important in the arts community: a place to exhibit one's work. "A lot of people don't have any opportunity to exhibit what they do, and that's a shame. I have said 'No' to maybe four or five people" who wanted to exhibit, she recalls. She tries consciously to make the exhibition process as painless as possible for artists while still maintaining her standards of quality.

Ms. Huntley believes that in general, artists need a facility like the Garden Studio because they are unwilling or unable (or both) to become involved with selling their work. "It's not the nature of the creative person," she contends. "Artists do well as being self-employed on the producing end of things. Their problems begin when it comes to showing their work." An artist can bring his or her work to a place like Garden Studio, leave it there, and get back to production and creativity. "It's not that I think there's anything wrong with selling," she observes, "but it becomes so time-consuming, and that changes the nature of the work."

As there is obviously some need in crafts for operations like Jinx Harris's that enable interested craftspeople to be involved in direct selling, so there also is some need for places like Garden Studio that make it possible for artists to devote much of their time to their art. Garden Studio is but one kind of a stationary exhibit space, distinguished from most other galleries by its lack of pretension and rural location. More representative of the genre, perhaps, are the more elaborate galleries of Boston's fashionable Newbury Street or New York's East Side. They perform the same function as Garden Studio, but for a different category of artists, clients, and amounts of money. In contrast to them, Garden Studio is more accessible, more populist.

Yet the clientele of Garden Studio defies description, being neither New York elitists nor the great unwashed. Ms. Huntley recalled the experiences of some of her artist friends, jewelers from Venice (Italy). "They were in New York, and selling nothing. They came down here and did great, and nobody could understand it. Friends said, 'Well, Emily, you don't expect that anybody here's gonna buy that stuff because it's surrealist, it's really way out there, and expensive!' They sold fifteen dollars' work in a year and a half in New York. Why did they sell it here? I don't know; and they sold to all kinds of people. They sold four thousand dollars' worth each year."

Garden Studio's low profile in no way implies a lack of seriousness either about its business or its art. The gallery is a beehive of activity, experimenting with a range of different kinds of shows (a sampling: Women's Art, Boys' Club Show, a jewelry show) and related activities like seminars. While she realizes that she is not directly supporting hoards of artists, she also knows that she is making an important piece of contribution for many, and that the existence of Garden Studio has altered the local buying community as well. More people in Greensboro have more contact with the arts because of Garden Studio.

The quality of the art at Garden Studio generally runs high. Ms. Huntley, herself an alumna of the highly regarded Rhode Island School of Design, simply couldn't see it any other way. She also points out, "All the great collections started in somebody's house —there was Robert Lehman, the Phillips Collection in Washington, and the Peggy Guggenheim Collection in Venice."

For herself, Ms. Huntley is interested in the development of Garden Studio and in furthering her own work, which recently has focused on drawing. She is profoundly interested in the contact the gallery gives her with others, both artists and buyers. It disturbs her when people tour through Garden Studio without saying hello. The gallery as she has established it is a people business, and that's the way she would like to develop it.

LINES OF COOPERATION—A LEAGUE

Garden Studio brings artists a bit closer to one another than the independent shops they run themselves. In many cases, artists have brought that contact another step closer by banding together to form guilds or leagues. Some of these provide support services that are quite extensive. For example, the Piedmont Crafts Guild has a gallery that exhibits members' work, and runs a large annual show. The Guild's home is literally a home, a large, gracious house in downtown Winston-Salem, North Carolina. Guild membership helps build an artist's credibility and reputation as well as provide a sales outlet, but joining is not simply a matter of sending off a check to cover dues. With 520 members the league is growing increasingly selective. In a recent round of applications, a jury approved twenty-two of the ninety-nine applicants for membership. Twenty of those had college degrees in arts (either a bachelor's or master's).

The support role played by the league is unclear, but some information supplied by its director, Lida Lowry, helped place it in perspective. About a third (215) of its members are full-time producing crafts-people, about a sixth are full-time teacher-professionals, and the rest (about half) are part-time. She did not have complete data on the whole membership, but knew that most of the new members belonged to three or more organizations like the league. She mentioned the names of some other groups and shops in the region and concluded, "If you want to make a living today in crafts, you have to belong to all of these."

League members control it, in theory at least, but Ms. Lowry believes that, "Professionals want an organization to represent them but they don't have the time to run it themselves or the inclination. They like to have a hand in governing but that's not what they want to do with their time." She believes that group members do want and need an organization that helps them sell their work.

Ms. Lowry sees the job of helping craftspeople sell their work largely as a process of education to develop public appreciation for the work being done. Piedmont holds workshops for members and runs slide-lecture shows to expand public exposure to professional crafts-people. Ms. Lowry fears the organization is not per-forming as well for part-timers who need representation, but she believes that the full-timers, at least from the viewpoint of her organization, deserve more support.

As far as prospects for further cooperation among craftspeople are concerned, Ms. Lowry echoes the senti-ments of Bill Sevrens: "I don't think people want it.

The creative process, the production process seems
to get slowed down when people are in contact with
one another. It's okay, I suppose, for the beginning
craftspeople. Before they reach a degree of skill and
confidence in their craft, they need this kind of community." Emily Huntley holds basically the same viewpoint: "Art is a solitary thing."

In spite of these antico-operation sentiments, various
forms of co-operation among craftspeople are beginning
to emerge, and some are thriving. One form of such
co-operation is an expansion of the guild concept, in
which craftspeople rent work spaces in one large building. A fledgling example of such an endeavor is located
in Winston, within walking distance of the Piedmont
gallery. The North Carolina League of Craftsmen,
occupying a massive (50,000 sq. ft.) renovated freight
terminal, has a large gallery space on its ground floor,
and another for seventy people upstairs. Spaces that
are "undeveloped" rent for $15 per month; "developed"
spaces go for $20.

When I visited, about half the spaces were rented.
None of the renters were full-time craftspeople, but
many hoped to be. Craftspeople there remarked on
the role the league has played in developing their work.
They can get out of the house, have access to better
work space than at home, and work uninterrupted.
When they want to take a break, they can usually find
someone to talk to. Rent is reasonable enough, and
the gallery downstairs helps sell what they make. The
overall operation is being held together with chewing
gum, a few workers who draw CETA salaries, and much
energy from a local philanthropist, but it seems to be
holding its own. It projects an ambience, and attracts
enough customers to make it seem fairly lively.

NETWORKING

The philanthropist and the CETA people, Lida Lowry, Elizabeth Huntley, and Jinx Harris emerge in all these co-op ventures as keystone figures between the arts community and the public. Similar roles are possible in other kinds of work—a *Boston Globe* article described the efforts of a woman who organized a musician's co-op in New England to help classical musicians find work.[2] All these efforts share some coordination of artists and some cultivation of public appreciation for the art. They often result in specific physical locations that further concentrates the artist-public interaction.

It also seems that the network people constitute a special kind of craftsperson, a maker of organizations and connections, a strange mix between host(ess), philanthropist, arts patron, teacher, student, and confessor. One especially noteworthy attribute of the species is its own high level of satisfaction. The networkers are a special breed and a happy one.

More extensive forms of cooperation are possible, particularly in two directions: shared residences for craftspeople and more tightly organized groups. Both have the appeal of cutting work costs, providing functional space, access to shared facilities at low cost, as well as access to people. Workspace is a big issue, as many crafts and arts pursuits need a kind of space better provided in industrial-type buildings than in traditional residences. Old factories and warehouses have strong floors to support kilns and machinery and may also have large windows. Perhaps more important, they also have atmosphere.

Following are descriptions of two different approaches to extended cooperation among craftspeople: the brief story of a building that was "recycled" from industrial uses for artists' housing, and a profile (presented in the form of a group interview) of a pottery co-op.

WORKING AND LIVING

As considerations of traditional business entail some concern for offices and physical plant, so considerations of people who make a living through the fine arts has eventually touched on some discussion of workplace. Many artists and craftspeople do their work at home, and although this can be very appealing and a key part of their approach to work it can be very difficult. Few residences have the trappings or amenities that lend themselves to a combined workplace and residence. Residences need very special qualities to function as workplaces, and artists' needs are particularly demanding.

Yet the idea of some sort of combined housing for artists and others who work at home is quite appealing and part of a solid and lengthy tradition of artists' communities. A community makes a neat balance for artists' individuality, providing a base of intellectual exchange and criticism and needed motivational and psychological support. In extreme versions the community idea has evolved as a real community, with people living and working closely together, perhaps in the same projects. Some communes have developed thriving businesses to support themselves, and some have been in the arts or crafts, but for most the work seems to have been secondary to the being of the commune.

The utopian communities of the nineteenth century were concerned with their work. A wide variety existed and in a wide variety of forms, some suggesting possible models for development in the future. Elbert Hubbard's turn-of-the-century group of "Roycrofters" in East Aurora, New York, for example, might have been a fore-runner of WPA-type economic development that centered on meaningful work.

Hubbard was a social critic-publisher-jack-of-all-trades who published a magazine (*The Philistine*) and some books in an operation that at one point employed some 175 people. He started alone but kept his doors open to anyone seriously interested in the work, which consisted mostly of very complicated and artistic book-binding and "illuminating" or illustrating. The group produced books of an astonishingly high quality in an atmosphere of intensive introspection into the meanings and possibilities of work.

Latter-day arts communities have sometimes centered on a school, like the famous Black Mountain College in North Carolina, or around Bohemian districts of a town, but the image of shared residence has remained alive. One recent experiment in shared residence is the re-cycled Chickering Piano Factory in Boston, which has been made over into residences for artists. The case of the Chickering Factory underscores the potential of such projects and the extreme difficulties of getting them off the ground.

THE CHICKERING PIANO FACTORY

Simeon Bruner first conceived the idea of recycling the massive (220,000 sq. ft.) Chickering Piano Factory into apartments when he was working in the building as a contractor in June 1971. Trained as an architect at Yale, he saw the potential of the then-dilapidated and financially troubled building to provide architecturally interesting and economically viable housing. He was impressed by the building's structural integrity and by the possibilities that its strength provided for design flexibility.

Bruner teamed up with Bob Gelardin, a friend with a background as a city planner from MIT, to try to market the building. Together, they came up with the idea of using the building for artists' housing. Its size and scale, the minimal number of supporting walls, the flood of natural light through numerous windows, and its high ceilings seemed to offer a potential for combined living and work spaces that artists, sculptors, and architects would find very attractive. A number of the building's pre-recycling occupants, in fact, were artists and craftspeople who found the building appealing solely as a workspace (some artists also lived in the building). Bruner and Gelardin also expected that emphasizing artists as their tenant community would enable them to minimize expensive architectural frills; they wanted to make the housing affordable and allow tenants to personalize their apartments to a large extent.

The two spent the summer of 1971 conducting a comprehensive market survey of the artist community, contacting local groups, reviewing mailing lists, and doing a considerable amount of interviewing. They concluded that over half the 5,000 artist households in the Boston area would consider moving for the right combination of more space and moderate rent, and that 70 percent of the artists' households preferred combined living and workspaces such as the Chickering building could offer. Armed with the survey, they began serious and complicated negotiations with the then-owner, local funding sources, and tenant groups.

Its owner was only too happy to unload the building —he owed money to four mortgagees and four years of back taxes to the city. Community support, however, was less than enthusiastic. The Boston Visual Artists' Union, the most promising organized potential tenant group, sympathized with the plight of the dozen artists and craftsmen located in the building whose work would be disrupted by the rehab work. Promises of priority in later tenant selection and long-term subsidized rents did not move the BVAU, and the organization voted (though not at all unanimously) to withhold formal support for the project.

Funding sources also presented a dilemma. Federal sources were not interested in any experiments, and the high prevailing commercial rates kept Bruner and Gelardin from even visiting a bank. The two directed their efforts to the Massachusetts Housing Finance Agency where, though they felt they were not quite met with open arms, they did at least find open doors and open minds:

"Agency standards had been based on new buildings," Gelardin observed. The MHFA expected the building to adhere to standards for new buildings, but the architect-developers argued strongly for a different set of standards that took its rehabilitation into consideration. The rehab standards they advocated were not necessarily lower, but different, largely because of the different needs of the projected tenant group. Many rehab standards involved simply rejecting work that is traditionally assumed in any building. The architect-developers questioned every aspect and asked a lot of questions that often get neglected. The MHFA, in return, questioned all the shortcuts, but acquiesced in a number of key cost saving issues such as:

Floors, which were in a state of significant disrepair, were patched rather than replaced.

Support columns were improved only to the degree necessary for structural solidity. Granite columns

were not sandblasted. Wood columns were reinforced with
an unfinished, rustic strapping. Brickwork was not re-
pointed to perfection.

Elevators were repaired instead of replaced

Piping and electrical lines were left exposed, with con-
duits running in bright metal tubes along brick walls.

The architect-developers also saved money in the open
space nature of the apartments, which required fewer
interior walls and the finishing work that goes along
with them. They connected the existing brick chimney
with the new heating plant and implemented a drain-
waste-vent system that served two, rather than the
usual one, unit. In replacing the roof, they added
dormers in the twenty-one top-floor apartments.

They balanced all the cost-cutting measures with
some features aimed at their tenant community: tack-
board walls in all the units, oversized doors, electrical
outlets mounted high for spotlights, a community gallery
in the entrance lobby, and the full development of the
courtyard into a landscaped park space. The fruit
of their labors has shown up in close-to-full occupancy,
tenant satisfaction, and awards from the Boston Society
of Architects and the Boston chapter of the American
Institute of Architecture.

Suzy Sicard, the building's manager, thinks the piano
factory is not free of problems. Many tenants are put
off by the surrounding neighborhood, and the building
has its share of intertenant squabbles and of conflicts
with the management. Artists living in the building
complain about noise leakage and about the minimal
financial success of the building's gallery space. Ms.
Sicard does feel, however, that the building is "not the
worst" she has seen, and points with some pride to the
low vacancy rate (five apartments of the 174 were vacant

when I visited in July 1975) and the overall condition of the building. She feels that the building's marketability hinges on the subsidized rents (one apartment she showed me rented for $124 to people with incomes under $6,000, $184 to people with incomes under $8,050, and $340 at market rates), and that the unsubsidized apartments are the slowest to rent. "But many of our 'market' tenants intend to stay in the building," she explains. Ms. Sicard pointed out that the living-working nature of the spaces minimized security problems in the building and showed off tenants' doors that had been decorated and personalized.

The architect-developers incorporated community and tenant input into the design and construction of the inner courtyard and the operation of the gallery space. Since the tenants share many interests, there is a fairly high degree of activity in the building. The building has also added somewhat to the strength and unity of the South End neighborhood in which it is located. Some tenants are involved in community projects and activities.

Architecturally, the building provides an object lesson in low-budget design. Because of its success, it has made recycling more palatable to other investors. Bruner and Gelardin are currently working on a mill in Hudson, New York, that is being funded by HUD—they feel certain that HUD is backing the project only because of their track record and the initial successful gamble taken by MHFA. But they don't feel recycling has a carte blanche among funders and agencies.

CLAY DRAGON POTTERY STUDIO

Besides a more communal living arrangement than in Piano Craft Guild, another way of organizing the work

of artisans is in a work co-op like those described in the
following chapters of this book. This arrangement
is notable for its rarity, but a few such groups do exist.
One, the Clay Dragon pottery studio in Cambridge,
Massachusetts, was just getting started when this book
was being written.

When I visited, the Clay Dragon Studio had not yet
opened. They were well along, however, in preparing
their rented "industrial space" for metamorphosis into
a studio and gallery. The walls were painted, a few
tables had been made, and some potters' wheels were
placed to take advantage of the natural light coming
in from the many windows.

The group of ten potters was taking things slowly
but quite surely, just as they had in their months of
livingroom meeting before they had rented the space.
Four dusty, perspiring members of the group took a
break from their work to tape the interview, and as the
conversation grew animated, it became impossible to
distinguish one voice from another. The four voices
appear below as one amalgam—not a unison melody,
but a tight harmony.

The interview began with an inquiry into the joining-
up process the last recruit of the group encountered.

WR   What was the process of coming into the group
     like? I remember the meeting that I went to they
     were doing a lot of haggling over this.

CD   It's all decided by consensus; any one person can
     stop the process. You come and meet with the
     group and then with individuals, one at a time.
     If anyone has doubts, they meet again and again.

WR   What was it like? Was it like a regular job inter-
     view?

CD   It could've been, but I kept telling myself it wasn't.

I could have gotten very nervous, but I wasn't in that subservient a position, it wasn't that my living depended on it.

WR Did people in the group go out of their way to make it less like a straight interview?

CD Yes, they did. It's an awkward situation, an uncomfortable situation because you're judging another person. It had nothing to do with the kind of pots people made, with whether or not they were good; we didn't even look at each others' work until months after we started.

WR Why was that?

CD Because that wasn't important. What was important was that people be able to work together.

WR It seems in that context that it might be even harder to do a job interview because you're not just looking at someone's skill, you're trying to judge their personality. I think it would be a lot more traumatic to have your personality rejected than your skills.

CD My feeling was actually just the opposite. If people had said, "her personality just doesn't fit with this group," fine, I can live with that.

WR So, in all the interviewing, there must have been some people who didn't get in. . . . On what grounds?

CD Who knows? Well, some of it was fairly clear. There was one person who came in, and everyone just felt, "No," because of the way she was. But with most people it was a more complicated, drawn-out procedure. Usually what would happen was that two or three of the members of the group would have reservations, and they would want to keep meeting with the person until they finally decided.

WR   And how many meetings did it take you before you joined the group?

CD   Three evenings, and I met with two members who weren't sure about me for dinner. Actually, my space in the group was the hardest because it was the last one. Everyone wanted something that wasn't yet in the group—a superstar.

WR   So the process you went through was especially difficult. Earlier on, you mentioned another thing that sounded difficult, and for everyone. You talked about making sure that people were committed to the group idea, and to clay. How do you go about ascertaining that kind of thing. Did it have to do with whether people would work here full-time or part-time; according to their commitment for hours?

CD   No, it was more just in attitude. Commitment was in people's wanting seriously to explore, in terms of their feeling, not a time commitment. We didn't want people who would dabble.

WR   So, among the ten people who are each paying $62.50 each month for the space here, some people are going to work full time but others are going to come in part time on evenings and weekends.

CD   But it is a real commitment to get into, it's more than just $62.50 a month. There was an initial investment, too, and an investment in time as well. Building the studio like we're doing now, for example, takes a lot of time and involvement.

WR   I hadn't really thought before about what happens, what the difference is between starting a group like this, and maintaining it once its gotten off the ground. It looks like starting it is really something special.

CD   Sure. Money is just about the least of it; it's

coming here every day and making these tables,
that I hate to do. It's very frustrating. But then
a lot of it is very satisfying too, like sweeping the
ceiling and getting the place cleaned up and ready
to open. It takes time.

WR Is there a lot of anxiety to get into production, or
are people resolved to however much time it takes.

CD Well, it hasn't been too bad until today anyway.
I hadn't touched clay in months, but I did today
and it made me really want the opening to come
sooner, sooner, sooner.

WR So how long has it all taken? What have you
done?

CD We spent almost a month cleaning; it was in-
credibly dirty. Then we spent a week painting,
it was a fantastic job. Then we built all the tables,
the ware racks, the benches, the wall, the bathroom. Everything that's here we made.

WR It sounds like an awful lot of work to me, not just
the physical effort but the amount of time people
put into it. I hate to be mundane, but how did
you manage to support yourselves during all this?

CD Well, only three of us have full-time jobs, and the
rest have part-time work. One of the full-timers
is a teacher, one works in an art supply store, the
other has time on weekends and evenings. A
few of us are waitresses, and there's a taxi driver,
and all of those can change their hours around
depending on how the pottery work goes. One of
us is a false-tooth maker, and she works half-time.

WR So all of you can pretty much chop back hours
when you want, or work evenings or days depending on how things are going here. It sounds like,
after you open, you'll be able to arrange the studio
here so that there are people here whenever you

think they should be. Do you have a schedule worked out to take that into account?

CD We haven't given a lot of thought to that yet; it's one of the millions of things that we'll get resolved in the fall. I don't see it as a problem, we'll figure it out along with everything else.

WR Did you settle on a formal framework yet, a structure behind all this flexibility? Is there a legal form that you've chosen, for example?

CD We're a nonprofit corporation, of which most of us are directors. There are other directors, too, who aren't part of the working group. We have to spend some time writing up the bylaws, but we are chartered.

WR Aside from the formal structure behind the flexibility, how do you deal with it personally? There's a lot of variation, it seems, among the amounts of hours you put in, and in the effort and commitment to the group. How do you work it out without getting angry with each other or feeling guilty, or feeling like martyrs?

CD Well, some of us have put in a lot more time than others, but we've tried to resolve the conflicts as we go along and it's been all right. We recognize that the group means different things to different people, and that's O.K.

WR So you've resolved conflicts in amounts of time people put in not by mandating that everyone work the same amount of hours, but by trying to legitimize the differences. . . .

CD By doing a lot of communication, and by legitimizing the differences. It's not easy, but there are some of us who are very good at keeping a discussion going, at resolving difficulties and talking them through.

WR It is difficult to resolve problems, and I think
you're very fortunate if you have some members
who are good at talking things through. How do
you do in things that aren't problems, in the day-
to-day kinds of communication? How are you
as a creative co-op? Is it so difficult to get along
in this sort of thing? Why, given all the numbers
of potters in the world, are there so few pottery
co-ops?

CD Well, that's not quite right. In other parts of the
world, pottery isn't so much of an individual thing.
In the East, for example, there are whole villages
that do production potting.

WR I guess I mean more the New England tradition,
the Western tradition of doing things alone in
pottery. Aren't there real economies in having
ten people share the space, and the gallery?

CD It's not just economics. For example, it would be
tough to have a good kiln, because you have to
work in an all-concrete or noncombustible space,
an industrial space, and you can't find small
industrial spaces. They didn't want to rent us this
6,000 square feet without renting us another 6,000
square feet in back. We said, "Look, this place
hasn't rented in thirteen years! Rent it to us and
we'll fix it up." They did, but it wasn't easy. In
terms of a smaller group getting a small space,
there just aren't any around. We were talking
some about it yesterday and we just couldn't
figure out why more people don't organize. We
know a guy at the Cape [Cod] who has a kiln
bigger than ours will be, and he only fires it about
six times a year. That's absurd, to have such a
big, indestructible piece of equipment that so
much effort has gone into, that's used so infre-

WR quently. We plan on firing our kiln once or twice a week.

WR Then what did you conclude about why more people don't organize; that it was too much of a hassle for people? I know you've put a lot of effort into the group.

CD I think that's part of it, and then too, a lot of it has to do with the difference between art and craft: in a gallery, you'll see the work of individuals, of one person making a statement rather than a tradition of something that is considered beautiful that many people have made.

WR Will people here at Clay Dragon work together on potting, or will they continue to produce pots as individuals?

CD We'll work as individuals, but I think people are going to be influenced by other people. We'll be able to get reactions from other people, and learn from each other.

WR You seem pretty well settled in this, but it seems more to me like another one of those things that only works itself out when it happens.

CD There's been a lot of that, and it's generally been pretty helpful as time goes on. I mean, in the beginning there were so many unknowns. Now there are fewer unknowns, we really know more about where we are. The problems are so much easier to solve when you have just some of the answers.

WR One answer I'm especially interested in has to do with the start-up costs. How do you deal with that kind of unknown? How much has it cost you all so far, while you're still waiting on tables and making false teeth?

CD About $1,000 each includes six months of rent

and materials for the kiln, which is quite expensive. Some of us have lent others some of their money, and one of us, the taxi driver, has been trained as an accountant, so he's helping keep all this straight.

WR That seems like a lot of money, but I guess it really isn't all that bad if you take into consideration what it would cost for one person to open up a shop. I'm beginning to see another problem here with working with a group, though, beyond the "creating together" issues: how do you deal with all the joint money decisions especially when people aren't always here to participate? Do you go ahead, and ask questions later?

CD It's basically a matter of trust. Part of the decision that you make in working here is to trust other people to be competent in the decisions they make, whether they have to do with making pots or going out to buy something.

WR Come on, now. You're making it sound just a bit too easy. Don't you ever get on each other's nerves, don't you get angry with each other?

CD Of course we do, but I think we're usually able to resolve those kinds of problems and have that kind of trust because we understand each other's compulsions. For example, in building our kiln now I'm getting very edgy because I want to see it done, but it's taking a long time because one of us wants total perfection in the way the bricks are laid. It's important, but not *that* important. Still, I would never say anything because like all of us, I have fits of perfectionism too. Besides, he's got to get the bricks right soon.

CHAPTER THREE

A New Slant
to Old
Professions

The professions have traditionally been havens of work
that people designed for themselves. Professionals
have long been able to design tasks within their jobs,
to carry out a tonsillectomy, a root canal, a corporate
audit, or a building design in whatever ways they saw
fit, pretty much free from supervision. Moreover,
professionals have traditionally had high enough pres-
tige and salary levels to be able to schedule their work
as they chose, and active professional organizations
that helped define and protect their prerogatives.

In a way a professional might be viewed as a kind
of craftsperson, highly trained and educated, and
usually deriving much satisfaction from his work.
Like crafts, the professions have welcomed a complete
kind of personal input from practitioners.

More recently, however, the situation as detailed on
the following pages by Ken Kruger for architecture is
typical for other professions. Parallels and analogies
can easily, perhaps too easily, be drawn for law,
accounting, medicine—even for writing. The implications for the kind of work that is available in the professions is ominous: it becomes increasingly more

difficult for people to find a variety of different kinds
of work involvements as work is defined more bureau-
cratically.

Watching the professions bureaucratize (unioniza-
tion is one example of the paths they may take, and
justifiably as people seek to protect what they have)
seems kind of like watching the world's oil reserves
diminish—inevitable, inexorable, and ironic with respect to what people actually seem to be doing with
their time. While the professions offer shrinking
possibilities for varying levels of personal involvement,
more people spend more time in school, raising their
expectations for what a job should deliver in terms
of satisfaction.

Yet it is still possible to find satisfaction within the
professions, even if one is not a senior partner; and
some of the organizational approaches being taken for
professionals seem quite promising. The Open Design
Office, for example, has approached architecture in a
way distinctly its own, a way that begins with its members. And it has found a useful way to cope with
economic ups and downs. The McCarthy-Towne
School and the Wilson-Burnstein Law Collective offer
approaches as groups to the issues of their own professions, and the individual planning consultant depicts
the joys and sorrows of pursuing a profession without
the support of a group. Meanwhile, the trials and
tribulations of traditional practice are well exemplified
in the profession of architecture, which seems to be at
the low end of the effects of inflation, recession, and
materials shortage. The following profile touches
on how these realities have affected the practice of
architecture.

THE ARCHITECT

He answers the door himself now; the receptionist's
desk is within view from outside the door, but it is too
neat, and dusty with disuse. Some things have not
changed—he is dressed for work much as he must have
been years ago, with sleeves rolled up and a grey shop
apron protecting a clean, white shirt. But the office
obviously has changed. Although it is well into the
afternoon, it has the vacant feel of an office whose staff
has gone out to lunch. In fact, it is a long, long, lunch
from which they may never return and for which they
may not be able to pay.

The Cambridge office of the architectural firm of
Kruger, Kruger and Albenberg exists now only in a
skeletal form. Ken Kruger answers the door and the
telephone, too, as secretarial help has gone the way
of the drafting staff—elsewhere, to other offices, other
professions. The firm has not had a contract document
for a job in over a year, and he is spending his time on
developing—buying and renovating multifamily homes.

Ken's position is typical of that of too many architects,
all victims of a near halt in new building construction,
inflation, and tight money. It seems most work now is
in the area of big projects. The few clients that have
money are the big ones least affected themselves by the
economic crunch. Their league is a complex one re-
quiring a large entry fee in terms of job development:
it takes time, resources, and money to find out who they
are and what they want. Having some lead on what they
want (and keeping in mind that they won't tell just anyone), it takes more resources and money to develop a
proposal to present to them. Where once a simple scale
model and a few pages of text were adequate, movies
with sound are becoming de rigeur. Presentations of proposals (especially to municipal and other governmental

clients who comprise a growing sector of the market)
are becoming almost theatrical, representing an investment in resources and money that only a large firm can
manage. "It's the old story that it takes money to make
money," Ken observes, "and small firms have less money,
can borrow less money, and can absorb the loss of a
rejected proposal less easily.

"The jobs seem to be bigger, too. The kind of work
that's around now, what there is of it, really requires
the services that a large firm can provide for support,
services like engineering, planning, and environmental
work that can't be worked out in a two-architect firm."
Small firms can build coalitions with other small firms
to carry out a specific proposal, but a firm that already
embodies all those networks has a clear advantage.

A Harvard Business School case study of architecture, "The Architecture Profession: An Industry?"[1]
notes that "[m]ore and more firms are incorporating
and some are even going public."[2] The study points
out the link that some firms have made with related
professional firms like engineers to offer broader
services and the buying up of some firms by conglomerates. Statistics used in the case show decreases
between 1962 and 1972 for smaller firms, for both the
individual practitioner and partnership forms, and a
growth in the corporate form.

1962	1972		
80	75.2 %	of firms ≤ 10	employees
92	87.1 %	of firms ≤ 3	principals or partners
80	77.9 %	of firms ≤ 3	architects

Large architectural firms have an edge over small ones for certain kinds of projects, especially in marketing services and for large projects that entail complex support services. However, the case contends that "in architectural practice there are no apparent economies of scale."[3] It is not, therefore, that large firms offer more efficient operations, but that they are better able to compete for clients in the shrinking marketplace and better able to manage related services.

For an individual architect, that evolving work environment (or at least, what is left of it in architecture's current financially reduced state) is located in large firms. This mere shift in the locus of the work setting would not be so meaningful if it were not accompanied by a complementary change in how the work is carried out. The larger firms allow architects to do lots of design work, but organize it to give only the most experienced architects control over the whole process. "Unless you're the job captain, or the main designer," Kruger claims, "your work will be tampered with a lot—it might even be so limited that you're just drawing what someone else has designed." Tampering with an architect's work, the norm in large firms, is tantamount to sacrilege, the most obnoxious kind of back seat driving, and yet because of the organization of work they must endure it.

The problem for architects begins with the reduced number of small firms. Given their preferences, one would suspect that they would stick with small firms if they were economically viable. In the pressures of the current economic environment, however, only the fittest survive, and for the current conditions it seems that bigness is a prerequisite for fitness. Even without economic pressures, however, there would be little optimism for small firms.

Ken Kruger believes that the growth of large firms and proliferation of links with conglomerates with no other ties to building and design in some ways augurs well for the architectural profession. "On the plus side, it means that architects can be involved in projects of a much larger scale and have more influence on the design environment. The planning of new towns is one example of this. Also, links with conglomerates ought to mean that architects will begin to have some influence in industrial design, an important social area that pays little attention to us now. Finally, it should also be possible in a large firm to do more architecture, to worry less about financing, public relations, and sales."

Links with conglomerates can lead to some dilemmas, though, and there doesn't seem to be any ready solutions for them. For example, if an architectural firm's corporate umbrella produces building materials (as some of them do), it could be difficult to arrive at an objective choice of the best material for a project. In a different vein, corporate overseeing, however gentle, of the time-honored relationship between architect and client, forces a difficult answer to the question of whom one is working for.

"On the negative side," Ken notes, "you no longer have the final say. Everything you do is subject to veto. Most professionals are very serious about their work, but I think it's even more so in architecture. Most people may not be at all interested in 'great architecture,' but architects genuinely are.

"If you're in I. M. Pei's or Ben Thompson's [two large firms], you will spend a lot of time on preliminary design. I can't do that here—I have to do my own PR, produce working drawings and worry about making ends meet. In a big firm, though, they'll put you at a drafting table and let you design. But, unless you're

the job captain, or the main designer, your work will
be tampered with a lot—it might even be so limited that
you're just drawing what someone else has designed."

"A guy who's been at Skidmore [another large firm]
five years, who's fully licensed, will still have his work
tampered with. The guys who work under the main
designer are generally unsatisfied—they're marking
time. They want to have the last say, and they want
to spend their time on important creations, not toilet
stalls. A large firm is good for people just out of
school—it gives them broad experience and contacts,
and it needs inexperienced people more than a small
firm."

Some "natural" forces in the building industry will
always limit large organizations. First of all, the
vagaries of a profession whose normal business experience is boom or bust may be too much for large
corporations that need to have some stability and
regularity. Second, though clients are currently "big,"
it seems there will also always be some small ones.
For them, there may well be advantages to working
locally with a small firm that understands the area, the
market, the laws, the banks. "Developers of smaller
projects want to be able to deal with an architecture
firm small enough so they can have ready access to the
boss when they want it.

"Also, small firms have flexibility, so that they can
pick up some projects that would fall between the slots
in a corporate net. A developer can come into a small
firm and bargain for the fee, for a piece of the project
or some equity in a way that large firms can't always
cope with and aren't likely to encourage." Ken is convinced there will always be small firms but worries
that there won't be enough to enable the profession to
offer different kinds of work for practitioners and to

carry out the kind of social responsibility that large firms seem to bypass: "Small firms are unable to do large projects; also, large firms are unable, in terms of their overhead, to do small projects. With too many large firms, the consequences for community architecture and social responsibility could be quite serious."

One organizational way of dealing with the big-small dilemma in the profession is suggested by a firm that has consciously parted with many of the traditions, the Open Design Office.

THE OPEN DESIGN OFFICE

"The economy" is a general abbreviation architects use these days to headline a lengthy list of specific difficulties plaguing the profession. Generally, economic recession has reduced the amount of money being put into construction. Specifically, everyone associated with construction and development suffers. Laborers and construction workers find themselves without work for months at a time. They may give up and try other kinds of work. For an architect with years of time invested in training, money invested in education and the development of a firm, and an often deeply personal commitment to this kind of work, job-switching would be a sacrilege.

Instead, the architects assume a conservative stance, taking what work they can get, laying off staff when they have to, and reducing their firms to a skeleton. Talk at a conference focuses, both in formal programs and in backroom scuttlebutt, on keeping one's head above water. Gossip carries a tally of layoffs from firms once at the forefront of activity in the profession. All matters of survival are matters of grave concern, and architects find themselves deeply involved with issues that only the old-timers remember confronting at any previous time: job-seeking, office management for economy, job development, sales. "The profession" has been forced to remove its tweed jacket (with the patched elbows), put away its pipe, and get involved with the once unprofessional matter of money.

The Open Design Office has partially succumbed to these forces, subleasing its office to a law firm while it weathers the financial storm. In contrast with the other reduced firms, though, Open Design maintains that the physical office space is not necessary if the work load doesn't warrant it. "The office" has become an association of persons connected by common attitudes about work, a group that coalesces in response to job requirements.

The law firm that has a short-term lease on Open Design's office space also has agreed to take their phone messages, and the messages do continue to come. Open Design holds meetings and works on small contracts and college teaching assignments. Work is done in members' homes; in a sense, the firm now exists as a cottage industry.

In a way, this condition is just a concentrated version of some of the fluctuations the group has already experienced. Membership in the firm has been fluid, reflecting the open boundaries of the office and the work of the moment. Open Design has always tailored itself to the work in which its members are engaged; different kinds of projects brought in different kinds of colleagues,

In the course of its four-year life, five members have relied on Open Design as a mainstay source of income, but have also found other work outside the firm to keep them busy and fed. Busy and fed is not, however, the most idealistic description of a professional career, and members of the group agree that they sorely miss the opportunity the group gives them to pursue architecture in a way in which they find comfortable and stimulating.

The Open Design Office's approach to architecture began with a perspective arising from the shared experience of its founders motivated by discussions in the Women's Architecture, Landscape Architecture and Planning (WALAP) group. Joan Sprague, one of the founders, recalled, "Those of us involved with WALAP shared the common experience of working as a minority of 1 to 4 percent in a male-dominated profession. We began wondering, 'What would a women's office be like?' and then we began to talk about really trying to do it."

Speculation about an office laid the groundwork for one member to approach the group with a specific proposal. She had been offered a job that she would not have been able to take on without enlisting some help. The size of the job staked the beginnings of the working group. The fact of the job forced the hand of the six women who had been discussing the possibilities for an office. "The job coalesced the idea," Ms. Sprague remembers. This is not to say that the job was viewed as a grant to fund the office but that the firm's creation enabled a group of loosely connected individuals to do some work that they would not have been able to take on as individuals.

Members of Open Design describe the dilemma of individual practitioners as typical in the profession, where an organization is necessary for all but the smallest projects. Ms. Sprague observes, "The firm gives us each a direct link to each other's expertise. An organization gives you the background and backup, it enables you to take on more kinds of work and gives psychological support, too." Having ready access to a diverse group made each group member more marketable as an individual. In addition, "having a firm sets out a self-fulfilling prophecy as the firm takes on a life of its own and begins to generate new work."

The women in the group wanted their own organization not only for these advantages, which some of them had already experienced, but also to undertake an experiment. Marie Kennedy, another member of the group, "had already been an employee, and I had been a boss, too. But I didn't like what happened in either position." A major reason for starting Open Design was to create an environment in which architecture could be practiced without bosses or employees but rather among friends and colleagues, as equals.

The shared perspective of the group as women also influenced their practice. A member noted, "In the past, gentlemen architects dealt with gentlemen clients. We felt that both ends of this equation are changing. We felt our early childhood conditioning as women influenced our work habits, and we wanted to test ourselves within a context of women, without any male influence."

The group structured the organization to embody a view of client relations that deviated from traditional practice, concentrating on working *with* rather than for a client. One group member observes, "We found ourselves agreeing that we didn't feel comfortable 'doing' a person's image. So often in the profession a client expects to just turn himself over to you. We have found it important to have continual input from clients.

"So many architects approach their work as artists, commissioned to do their specialty. Clients in that type of arrangement feel intimidated, thinking they 'should' like whatever the architect turns out. We thought there was a need to distinguish between art that people can take or leave and art that people don't have choices about, built art that people live in. I guess what we're talking about is a breakdown of the hierarchy between an architect and a client as well as between the members of an office, with each bringing to the project his or her own skills."

It's difficult to say which caused which, but the group's internal structure and method of management differs from standard practice in tandem with its approach to clients. In most firms, the people who solicit and agree to take on a job are usually not the people who actually work on the job. In fact, the people who work on a job typically have little choice about what they will work on. In Open Design, members "volunteer" for work. When a job inquiry comes in, two members of the group collect information on the project. They present it to other members at the office meeting. The group then decides whether to take a job based on consensus at the meeting. They have not taken on a job unless a member has expressed an interest in working on it.

The group's organization enables this sort of "piecework" approach to occur in its provision of payment only for work actually done. This pay-as-you-go view may not seem terribly innovative unless one realizes that in most architectural firms, salaried workers get weekly checks but partners (which is what members of Open Design are) get the rest.

Members ran Open Design less like an architecture firm than a research center: members who work on a project are paid at an agreed-on hourly rate roughly equal to what any office pays. The remaining funds are consigned by mutual agreement to overhead and payment for other work necessary to the continuity and goals of the office. (Incidentally, the group's initial hourly wage rates ranged from seven to twelve dollars an hour, depending on the comparable rate that a member could expect in a traditional firm.) Joan Sprague observes that the group "tended to raise the lower pay rates and reduce the high ones a bit" to follow through with their beliefs about minimizing inequalities of income.

Marie Kennedy points out that the group's financial structure made the organization more flexible. "They tell us in professional practice courses that it takes two or three years for a firm to get out of the red. Meanwhile, they're paying salaries and trying to generate a high volume. With our organization we needed no initial investment. Our 'risk time' (see bylaws in appendix) financed the office. Also now that things are slow we don't have a whole institution to keep running." (They figured that their overhead averaged five hundred dollars per month and that the largest piece of this except for rent was for phones.) The finances of Open Design gave it a greater capability to respond to the vagaries of available money. Equally important, the pay-as-you-go process meshed with the notion of volunteering (or not) for work which meshed in turn with the group's redefined relationships with clients. Close client contact and productivity-based remuneration grew out of opposite ends of a member's unpressured choice of her work.

In some of its approach to the design process, Open Design mirrored some of its views of client relations and definitions of work. "Architects and some students think that group work implies designing 'by committee,' " Ms. Kennedy recalls. "But of course that wouldn't work. We often work on things together and we try to be involved in each other's work. There is a lot of talking going on along the way. Ultimately, though, we get things done faster than in a traditional firm.

"In a traditional firm, design usually goes two steps forward and six steps back. You've got one person writing specs, another working on a site plan, another doing working drawings, and maybe another supervising everything. None of them talks to the others in a traditional firm; it seems that the hierarchical firm goes with people doing a lot of bluffing and competing. Without talking things out and keeping tabs on each other, it's likely that each person working on a project will go off on tangents. We may move more slowly than the hierarchical firms, but they have a lot of correcting work to do, and in the end they might be less efficient."

Joan Sprague thinks that within the process Open Design follows "our own creativity is enhanced by the organization." She believes that the organization served the creative interests of the members as individuals in its norms of mutual criticism and learning. "Each member is encouraged to ask the others for suggestions, opinions, and assistance."

Moreover, she points out that the group's high level of internal communication also led them to "be creative" about aspects of the work unrelated to design, to question standard operating procedures that normally go uncontested. The group discovered, for example, that they shared a fervent dislike for the inefficiency and ineffectiveness of putting their time into "working drawings," the plans on which it is said that architects spend 90 percent of their time. Open Design has experimented with and evolved working drawings that include photography and a simplified form design to encourage input from the contractor. This helps make the whole process more gratifying for both designers and contractors, both of whom can contribute their knowledge to the end product.

For an architect to take on the institution of working drawings and develop his or her own approach is the profession's equivalent of a doctor who considers trading in his black satchel for a backpack. In the case of Open Design, the new form proved itself to the external world and met the needs of the group, and the members realized that the existence of the group provided the current of conversation and confidence that enabled them to raise the issue in the first place. Marie Kennedy sums up the situation: "there was a tremendous potential for learning in the office."

They have developed their own accounting and job definitions to try to answer other questions that seldom get asked in traditional firms. Joan Sprague contends that this kind of self-analysis is a natural outgrowth of the group's original interests. "After all," she remarks, "we *are* designers. In the office we just turned our design skills toward our organization and the way we did our work." (A detailed chart on Open Design, prepared by Joan Sprague, included in an appendix to this book, provides more information on the firm and explores the uses of such charts.)

GOING IT ALONE—
THE PLANNING CONSULTANT

She is a free-lance consultant in planning, a field that offers fertile diverse ground for cultivation by generalists. There are a lot of very different kinds of work that go by the title "planning," most of the work she does interfaces in some ways with architecture. She has maintained a loose affiliation with a group resembling Open Design, but is mostly on her own.

The approach of consulting maximizes the diversity of planning by sanctioning "bouncing." Many other professions use consultants, too, and they all share a measure of transiency. There are other, less strenuous (and less lucrative) ways to "do" planning, but there is a certain appeal to consulting: it is always a learning experience, a challenge, a novelty. Many planners trace a long-term career path that includes intermittent stints of consulting mixed in with work in larger firms and governmental agencies.

She has opted for the consulting approach to planning, and she enjoys it immensely. It all may change when she gets a bit older and perhaps loses some of the requisite energy, but then again she may also grow still stronger. Now in her mid-thirties, she rides the crest of the professional wave. She is in demand, having painstakingly built a network of contacts that she continues to cultivate. She has helped create much of the demand for herself, and she designs each of her work arrangements with meticulous attention paid to the development of her current interests. She treats herself well in designing her work; that may be her chief motivation for doing it, except perhaps for her sense of exhilaration.

"I'm enormously comfortable working on my own. There's a thrill, an excitement. When I lived in New York I worked for some government agencies, some city agencies, and I did some teaching. New York was stimulating; there was so much going on and I tried to get involved in a lot of it.

"I made good money and kept very busy with work, and outside work, too. What finally happened was that I became full of New York—not angry or disgusted, just full, like after a rich meal. I needed to make a change—my move to Boston signified that I wanted a change in my career. I had been working as a planner in New York for ten years.

"When I moved here I supported myself by doing some work for the New York firms. It was all done by correspondence, very neat and clean. Meanwhile, I started developing other kinds of work. I was intent on doing research as an intellectual pursuit instead of just as a way to make money. I looked up a woman who had an article in the same issue of a journal that ran an article that I had worked on. We got along pretty well and started to do some work together.

"We spent a lot of time developing proposals—it was a good way to help us get our thoughts straight. We probably could have actually gotten funded—if we had pursued it hot and heavy, we could have gotten a grant in a year and a half or two years.

"It was about that time when I started doing some independent consulting. I knew some people socially who did consulting work, so I asked around and kept my eyes open. I called people and I went around to see them. That part of it is very time-consuming, and it's a gamble. You never know if it's better to drop in unannounced and keep your fingers crossed or to call ahead.

"I found that I really liked it. It's like you're perpetually job-hunting. That can be inhibiting to some people, but I thought it was fun. You have to learn the etiquette. You keep contacting people. You call up and ask what's happening. You never say 'Look, I'm out of work.' You play very cool and very friendly, and sure enough, things eventually turn up. (When they didn't, I went back to my friends in New York and got more work from them.) It's a balance you walk between bothering people and being familiar enough to turn up a job. I've gotten a couple of jobs over other people just because I was a household word for the contractor. It's funny; people will give you a job based on a few minutes' phone coversation even though they've never seen you.

"Some people get hung up on the insecurity that comes out of this kind of work, but I thrive on it. I used to send out probes for more work in the last few days of whatever job I was at because I had found that even the way I was doing it, it was true that work was easier to get if you already had it. Now I don't even bother with sending out probes because things always seem to work out for me. You need an enormous amount of optimism to do this, I suppose, but then again I think that the optimism you have creates its own results.

"One thing about this kind of work that I like most is the kind of jobs that you get. In this business, you only get work when something needs to be done. People hire planning consultants only when they're up to their ears in problems, or they can't figure out how to work things out on their own. You go in, and you're not window dressing. You've got a real problem to solve. My friends who have regular planning jobs with different government agencies and in the research firms say that the consultants who come in are the ones who get the most challenging work.

"I like the idea of having my work broken up into jobs. You contract, you do a piece of work, you get it done. So many planners work in positions—they don't have work, they have a position. Lots of them are very dedicated and they work very hard, but having a position and knowing that you're going to be there produces an enormous amount of stagnation. Then there's a few who aren't as wrapped up in the work. I think they have the feeling that as long as they're there, physically, in the

office, they're by definition doing work. It's all so safe
and so reliable. If you work at one of those places your
position is solid. You may never get to be boss, but
then again, they'll never fire you either.

"When I come in, I have a job to do and I get it done.
No position, just work. I know that the thing isn't
going to go on forever, and I've got to do a decent part
of it. My friends in the agencies never really finish a
job, but I get to have an ending to my work. Sometimes
I feel like the ending of a job is the best part. It's a
productive feeling; you've produced something. You're
up and out looking for other work, for something else
you can do and finish. When I worked in an agency, and
from what I get from my friends, it's still true: there is
very little beginning of work or completing work, only
continuing it ad infinitum, ad nauseum.

"On the other hand, I guess I would be less than honest if I didn't say a little about some of the problems of
doing work this way. In terms of the work itself, your
sense of accomplishment can get shot down pretty
quickly when it comes to the uses people may put your
finished product to. Sometimes your report just gets
ignored, as in cases where they've gone out and contracted research because some regulatory agency
forced them to or someone in their own bureaucracy
thought it would be a good idea. In those cases you
really are window dressing, and you may even be a tool
for who knows what ends. Of course, you're not stuck
there to worry about it but your ears may burn when
somebody waves your report around and uses the information in ways you would never want to be associated
with.

"Then, too, there are problems with money. I make a
comfortable living all right, but I mean here about the
etiquette of setting a fee. I generally set my fees by

what I know others get, but there are remarkable discrepancies in the fee-setting aspects. Business consultants, it seems, get enormous amounts of money. Some planners with little experience earn much more money than some with a lot of experience. The strangest thing is that it seems that, the higher your fee, the more credible you are. The firms that hire you seem to assume that you only ask for what you've gotten elsewhere and that what you've gotten elsewhere is an infallible guide.

"I set my fee fairly high just to keep in the running, but I used to think I wasn't worth what I was getting. Then, after I had been working a year, tallying up my own expenses, I began to realize what a tremendous deal I was for the people who were hiring me. I was costing those firms much less than any regular employee. I didn't get any benefits, any vacations. I had to pay all that myself, and it really adds up. I don't believe in life insurance so I simply don't carry any. Health insurance is a real problem, though: I don't have any. It doesn't really worry me, but I know I should have it. And it does worry my mother. I don't really take vacations—my mother says my whole life is a vacation. I take a lot of long weekends.

"I do most of my work at home. Work in an office is too regimented. I feel very together at home; I don't feel the need to go off somewhere and relax. I do need to have a whole day to work in, though, or I waste a lot of time. I need to be able to get up and know that I can plan a whole day for working, with only minor interruptions. I carve out days for different things. I try and book all my appointments for one day because, once I start traveling, a whole day is usually shot.

"It gets to be very intense working that way, but I find that I prefer it. I plunge into whatever I'm doing.

Then, too, I usually have to pull out and do something completely different for contrast. I find that at least once a day I need to get on my back. I need to totally divert a little in just about everything: I'll work really hard, then tend my plants; I'll read a technical journal, then a novel.

"I always have this little joke with people. They can't believe that if I'm at home, I'm really working. Someone will ask, 'Where's your office?' I'll say, 'I work at home.' And then I get the overtones, 'Oh, yeah, sure you do.' It's as if it weren't legitimate for people to be doing real work in their homes. Even offices that I work for don't seem to want to recognize that I work at home. People just recently began calling me at home for business reasons after I found out that some of my contractors were hesitating to bother me. I said to them, 'Look, this is a business. My home is like an office.' I get business calls now, and I'm beginning to get some of my business mail, too. Though I must confess that I take some delight, every now and then, in just letting the phone ring without picking it up. Bureaucracy depends on people answering their phones. To not be there is a luxury, and I like to indulge in it consciously every once in a while.

"I can't imagine why people have these feelings that work and home have to be separated. I made the decision three years ago that I wanted my work to be integrated with my regular life. It's a decision I feel comfortable with, but also that I have to keep reaffirming and clarifying because so much of what people assume separates home and work. I guess most people just don't have the opportunity—or take the opportunity—I guess is a better way to put it—to do things differently.

"I don't really mind that I have to keep reminding

people about my work at home, but I do mind the overtones that go with that because I'm a woman. I'm not
certain about this, but I think that I have to do more
explaining about my working at home because I'm a
woman. Somehow, it's more legitimate—but still not
completely—for a man to be working at home. I get the
feeling from some men, and some women too—and that
really irks me—that women who work at home are *really*
either taking in ironing or taking in men.

"Even that doesn't bother me quite so much as the
continuing process of definition and reminding I go
through with the man I'm living with. He is not a male
chauvinist by any stretch of the imagination, and yet
we're always having these discussions about my work
at home. Because I'm home, I'm supposed to be the one
who sees what food is there, to run out and pick up a
few things if we need them for dinner. After all, I am
there, and it all seems so convenient. I actually did this
a few times before I realized what was going on.

"I guess what got me to see it best was one day when
I was out and he stayed home. I was working on a very
difficult project, and I had to rush out early in the morning. At the end of the day, as I was coming back, I was
just assuming that he would have dinner ready and the
apartment straightened up. Of course, nothing had
been cleaned or cooked and in fact, there were more
things to be done because he hadn't picked up after
himself. I stood in the door, just looking, and when
he said, his first of the day to me, 'Ready to make
dinner?' I practically exploded.

"We talked it out for a long time. It had simply never
entered his mind that he should clean up. He took for
granted that he should have a share of things when he
was home, but it hadn't occurred to him to take over
when I wasn't there. That's where I started realizing
how much of my time in work days was spent in doing

little things around the house. I still do some of them
—a little vacuuming, maybe some dusting, but I always
try and ask myself first if there aren't other things I
should be doing first. He's making an honest effort,
it seems, to not just help out but to take some initiative
to see that work gets done, and things are gradually
coming around, but it's all very, very slow.

"The only other problem I have with working so much
at home is that sometimes the balance between work,
home, and privacy shifts to block out privacy completely. I see other people give up their privacy by
giving away so much of their time to work in an office,
and I don't want to do that. I believe that it's possible
to live your work so that it more closely approaches
your personal values and interests and, when it does
that, I think privacy gets very blurry, and that's good.
I also believe that the best way to find privacy is
through a kind of total immersion that you step out of
—to go for a bicycle ride, a long weekend, or whatever,
when you feel like it.

"I think that all these aspects of working are tied up.
For example, I think it's possible to approach work
with these views of privacy if you're doing work that
you want to be doing. I've finally reached the point
where I won't work unless there's something I want to
work on. There's no sense to all this independence
business if I go out and take on work that I really don't
want—I could be doing that sort of thing in an office.
What continues to amaze me is how difficult it is, even
for me as an independent consultant, to turn down work
that I don't want. I think it says a lot about the way
we're socialized to think about work. I know how easy
it would be for me to knuckle under to taking boring
work, and I can easily imagine how quickly people
working in offices get used to it.

"I'm also of the opinion that working independently

fits into a larger scheme of living on the consumer side.
I mean, I think a lot of people get steady jobs because
they've established their lives so they have to have a
steady income. They lock themselves into a pattern
of consumption first and then the work has to follow
from that. I'm aware that lots of people do have real
financial pressures and I don't want to minimize that,
but I also believe that people often take on more than
they really need to. It gets into a whole value system,
and it seems to me that people mostly accept it without
ever really thinking about it.

"Part of it, too, is that I don't think that in this country
we're able to manage money. It comes and goes and
people throw up their hands and talk about it as if it
were the weather. People fall into using credit, and
once they do that, they have to have a regular income.
I've never bought anything on credit. There are lots of
things I'd like to have and I can see that it could be a
convenience, but I don't want to trade my freedom for
convenience. I look at it this way: most people couldn't
go for a month, or for two months absolute maximum,
without a regular income. They have too many obliga-
tions. It makes our society overall remind me of the
early agrarian societies where people were enslaved
to the land. Now we're enslaved to the need for a
regular income.

"My work has gotten to a point now where I'm beginning to make some refinements that make a very big
difference. In this one job, I'm working in a longer
period of time so that I'm not just writing reports. I'm
able to stay around and see things get implemented,
even to work on getting them implemented myself.
We've become—the other consultants and myself—more
of an operating arm. We're not writing reports, we're
giving them information for programs—and they're

using it. Part of our job is to see that they use it. In some ways it's like being a staff person because we're there so often, and we know the people, and we're involved in most aspects of the project, but since I'm not a staff person and don't really have long-term interests in the work through a position, I can say things that no staff people can say. I'm not protecting my job as they are. I renew my contract with them every three months and I know I can leave without a second thought, so I can afford to be more frank than any of them.

"I have realized from this job that I do enjoy the support of a group. I like to do this work independently, but then I can also see how much more enjoyable it can be working with a group. You can learn a lot more, and there's a lot to be said for the psychological supports from contact with a group. My problem is that most group work that I know of is office work, and there we go again. It's structured, it's bureaucratic, it's in an office, you have a boss.

"I have been working on the side, over the years, with friends, to put together a group of our own. It got off the ground and did pretty well there for a while, but then the economic crunch hit and leveled us. We still meet regularly, but there isn't much to go on and we've pretty much kept our original jobs. We tried to have a nonhierarchical structure, but hierarchies seem to be created more out of personalities than structures, and we had some personality conflicts. We have remained fairly close, though, and having the group to meet with has meant a lot to me even if I haven't worked with it much directly. We trade ideas and contacts, and the social part of it is important to me, too.

"I think every once in a while about going back to school. A few people have told me to do it, to go ahead and get the Ph.D. while I'm still young. I think I could get a lot out of school now, but that would mean having to take time away from my work. In the long run it would probably be a very wise thing to do, but for now, I just can't think about it. I'm getting too much out of my work to seriously consider cutting it back. The only reason I really have to force myself to think about it is that it would give me more independence. Most of my contracts now are subcontracts from other consultants. With the doctorate, I'd be more able to go get my own contracts, and that would be worth a lot to me."

THE ALLSTON-BRIGHTON LAW COLLECTIVE OF WILSON AND BURNSTEIN

The collective represents in the legal profession what Open Design represents in architecture, but the groups differ considerably, as do the professions. The high level of activity in law is almost exactly opposite of the low level in architecture. Still, the conditions for beginning lawyers and architects are not all that different and many of the norms of professionalism are very much the same.

The law collective's digs clearly are not those of F. Lee Bailey; the decor tends more to sparseness than to luxury. The furniture is old and worn, and there is a noticeable absence of high-technology office paraphernalia like Xerox machines and IBM typewriters. The telephone, however, is busy, and the lawyers are on their toes.

This law collective, founded a year earlier by its principals Barry Wilson and Dan Burnstein, is one of about a dozen in the Boston area that occupy about seventy lawyers. Like many of the others, Wilson and Burnstein also rely heavily on the services of law students and paralegals.

Lee Goldstein, a member of the Project Place law commune who has been involved with law collectives for over five years (and who has written an excellent book on *Communes and the Law*, available from Project Place), traces their beginnings to the late 1960s when the number of jobs in law began to dwindle while the traditional organization of legal work came to be perceived with increasing distaste. This perception was sharpened by the inability of many law firms to accommodate the evolving political interests of new attorneys.

Dan Burnstein notes: "The essence of the beginning discussions of our group was that we were dissatisfied with traditional law practice. Rather than fit in with a regular firm we thought it would be more exciting, challenging, and rewarding to start a practice on our own. At the same time there was a real lack of openings in other firms. Then, too, we felt that we were not just attorneys but political attorneys. We wanted to apply our efforts at the most susceptible points of issues in Boston to make the most of our training."

For many groups, the choice of cases is particularly important because it enables them to play out their political beliefs. A number of the groups are very political, and some will accept a case only if it has some "political merit." Others maintain that simply providing legal services for people who couldn't otherwise afford them is in itself political. Wilson and Burnstein maintain a running argument about this which they have resolved (at least for the moment) by agreeing to each take divergent paths. Wilson takes many low-paying apolitical ("Band-Aid," Dan Burnstein calls them) cases, while Burnstein splits his time between high-paying apolitical cases and overt, voluntary political action cases usually in civil rights and through the National Lawyers Guild. Wilson has worked on the defense of some blacks who were arrested in a "disturbance" in South Boston and in other civil rights work and Burnstein has worked on aspects of bilingual education.

The "Band-Aid" approach should not be overlooked —providing legal services for low-income people affords an opportunity to provide simple, important help and to raise consciousness. As the reach of formal law has made itself felt in more areas to more people, the likelihood that a person will need legal services has markedly increased. Legal fees have risen to keep ahead of inflation, leaving many potentially at the mercy of inferior legal aid. Legal Services has helped matters, but not solved the problem.

Beyond the concern for politics, many collectives seriously restructure the traditional structures of legal practice. "In a large firm, you carry somebody's briefcase for five years before you even try a case," Lee Goldstein observes. The glut of law school graduates available apparently has helped rigidify the hierarchical design of work in law offices, creating what Goldstein terms a "feudal" work system. Partners are the lords, having access to the most interesting work; young lawyers, associates, are pages responsible for the less interesting chores; and secretaries are serfs just a notch above domestic animals. Within this feudal system, Barry Wilson describes another hierarchy of status attainment for lawyers, going from prep school to college, to law school, to the firm, then to partnership in the firm (after five years, perhaps), and then to managing partnership. "The point is," he observes, "that it never stops. For young lawyers who think they've made it, things can be very trying. I've seen lawyers, the big honchos in the big firms, cut a new lawyer down piece by piece with a vengeance. But what really got me even more was that the young lawyers sat there and tolerated it."

Many of the law collectives have begun with a more egalitarian work system affording members greater control over the work they do, even to the extent of simply eliminating the position of legal secretaries. Barry Wilson explains: "We don't have a legal secretary —we have five of them. Everyone is his or her own secretary." Wilson believes that the firm does not lose efficiency in the long run, and points out that not hiring secretaries enables them to hire more student lawyers. Most important, though, he and the others simply don't feel comfortable with the division of labor that comes with hiring secretaries.

As in the Open Design Office (the worker-run architecture firm), lawyers in law collectives volunteer to work. They choose the cases they wish to work on and they turn away cases they don't want. Cases may be rejected if no one is interested in them or if they lead the groups onto questionable political or social ground. Some groups, for example, seldom or never defend accused rapists. The ability to choose their cases at least allows lawyers to avoid cases they find repugnant, in contrast with traditional firms that accept all cases.

Wilson also believes there is an analogy between the craftsman's desire to work through a project from beginning to end and the desire of a lawyer to do likewise. He observes, "Without being involved in a case from beginning to end, you never get a real appreciation of what's going on, nor can you get really involved." In the collective, people work a case all the way through, usually discussing it with the other members but always having input into how the case progresses.

In traditional law practice, beginning lawyers seldom are able to work a case through, because work on a case may be divided among numerous lawyers and legal researchers. Within this division of labor the most interesting part of the work, trying the case in court, is reserved for the most experienced lawyers. In some firms, however, even the more experienced lawyers seldom get into the courtroom, as the firms may have a number of trials "aces." In large, urban District Attorneys' offices, beginning lawyers may spend years only screening arrests, while more experienced lawyers only try the cases in court. The larger firms may specialize to a great extent, and specialization may track a lawyer into bookwork. "Lots of lawyers don't mind this, some even like it," Wilson observes, "and as for those who do mind it, they can go elsewhere because there are plenty of other lawyers around these days to take their place."

The larger firms hold some definite advantages for clients with a lot to spend on legal fees. Armed with a sizable bankroll for support, they may approach a case by "papering to death" the other side. If the other side is small, they must devote a disproportionate amount of their time responding to "all that crap," as Wilson refers to it. The strategic position of the smaller firms is further complicated by their inaccessibility to IBM typewriters and in-house copying machines. Wilson and Burnstein have access to a copying machine, but so do the rest of the customers of the drugstore down the block. Even when there is no one in line ahead of them, it's still a ten-minute walk and an inconvenience.

Despite their lack of high technology office equipment, Wilson and Burnstein believe they do well for their clients. Wilson feels that judges usually see through "papering," and that the attention and preparation collective members give to their cases (a logical product of being able to choose one's cases) often gives them an edge. Besides, the clients they usually take on often are not the kind that get into "paper" cases. In

addition, the number of high-technology firms around
is limited, and more growth seems to be occurring in
firms organized like the collective or still more at the
margins. Wilson believes an increasing number of firms
operate out of people's apartments.

Clients attracted by their low fees, their dedication
to the work and their growing reputation also find at
Wilson and Burnstein a different approach to expectations of who they should be. "We try to demystify the
law," Barry Wilson explains. "We tell them all about it
and, when it's possible, teach them enough so they can
carry on by themselves.

"It sounds like it would be an easy thing to do, but
it's not. People come in and they seem to want somebody to look up to, somebody who can take over their
problems and solve them. They don't want to know the
law; they don't want to know why things happen the
way they do. They put themselves in this supplicant
position, lots of our clients call us 'sir' at the beginning.
I tell them 'I'm not a sir; I have a name. Call me Barry.'
It's as if they crave some kind of authority.

"It's easy as a lawyer to stand on the pedestal they
build for you, it's a great ego trip. They look at you
pie-eyed because, to them, you're this incredible thing.
It's very easy for you to become impressed with yourself. We try to say to them, 'Look, the law isn't magic,
and what we're doing isn't a miracle. Anyone can do
legal research, with a little bit of training.' We want
people to feel in more control of their lives and not to
see the law as this invulnerable, mysterious force. The
law isn't so complicated, it's just inaccessible to the
average person.

"It's not hard to be a lawyer, I hate to say it. We have
this one case, a dissolution of a partnership of musical
entertainers. We're negotiating the separating of musi-

cal equipment. My client could do this, and I told her so. But she's paying me to take the abuse for her, to give out the abuse. They're not big legal things—she's paying me to open my mouth. I've been opening my mouth for years and nobody gave me a dime, they just gave me a hard time."

The economics of the firm is rooted in an overall different approach to law: clients and cases are different than in firms that trade in corporate law. In addition, the members of the collective are not driven by the desire to get rich. "All of us want to make a living," Wilson remarks, "but none of us entered the field so that he could make a lot of money." He points out that they would make at least two times their current salary with Legal Aid, or three times as much with a private firm, and that their experience would make it entirely feasible to get a position in either.

High salaries or high overhead (their rent at the co-op is $150 per month), however, would weaken what they want *most*—to provide competent legal services at a reasonable cost. They believe they could charge much more, and tighten up their business practices (unlike many lawyers, they don't insist on a retainer before beginning a criminal case) to make more money if they wanted, but they're more interested in practicing law in their own way. Wilson remarks, "If corporate lawyers were paid what we get, they wouldn't show up for work. For us, the work comes first." They also believe that with the firm set up as it is they can earn enough to be comfortable.

The way the firm is set up differs from traditional practice, as do the choice of clients and cases. Wilson and Burnstein themselves each have contact with the firm's average hundred cases or so, often with one of the law students. Every case has some direct involvement from them, though the students are able to exercise considerable responsibility. The students get paid at the same hourly rate as the lawyers. Information flow is handled in informal contacts in the course of work rather than in formal meetings because they believe meetings are too time-consuming. "Time is our biggest resource," Wilson observes, and underscores their reluctance in wasting it.

Though they are somewhat experienced and not at all lacking for clients, Wilson and Burnstein do rely on outside help. Specifically, they have often found a need for opinions and advice on particular issues, and have gotten assistance from an older "left" lawyer and a younger politically active lawyer. "I think nothing of calling them up," Wilson comments. "But for them, we couldn't exist."

When I visited, the collective had been in existence for one year. Wages had reached a level of about a half of what members wanted, and they felt that was reasonable progress. The phone kept ringing.

THE McCARTHY-TOWNE SCHOOL

Here's a seemingly normal professional man, well dressed, sitting in an office whose clutter conveys the concern for getting things done first (and worrying later about tidying up) that one might expect of any lawyer, accountant, doctor, or school principal. Actually, this particular man is the latter, as vouched for by the titles in the book cases and perhaps more conclusively by the nature of the lunch he perches on his knee. Where but in a public school could one find the culinary daring to bring to the same styrofoam tray a small doughy pizza, some string beans, crushed pineapple, pink fruit juice, and a cookie?

The forces that have helped to create school lunches are also at work elsewhere in the school: in the scaled-down furniture that places adults in a surrealistic, Alice-in-Wonderland perspective; in the mobs of miniature human beings in bright clothing, all potential refugees from a peanut butter ad. In some schools the forces take a chilling twist, bearing witness to long-time friends calling each other by their last names in front of awed children who are supposed to listen, above all; or to reasonable adults reduced to tooth and claw arguments with waifs one tenth their size; or to adults—parents, teachers, and principals—pitted determinedly against each other for reasons an outsider would be hard pressed to understand.

Parker Damon, the principal at issue here, is in a position that would appear to add insult to the palate injury of school lunches, for he does not have access to the traditional consolations of power and authority open to most principals. Actually, the consolations that go with being the boss are, for many principals, marginal considering the headaches. Like dentists, most principals strike few friendships in their work. They are in a position of potential conflict with teachers, students, parents, and the higher-ups on the board of education and in the superintendent's office, all of whom seem to conspire to gang up and ambush a principal at the same time.

It's not so easy to ambush Parker Damon, but that isn't because he either evades or dominates well. Damon is not really the boss at the McCarthy-Towne School in Acton, Massachusetts. In fact, if word got out among the teachers there that he was carrying on like a boss, they'd probably confront him with it and possibly fire him if he didn't shape up. Damon's position seems tenuous indeed, but there is some argument to be made that his role of principal-as-facilitator ("co-equal and

Executive Agent of the staff" is how one of the school's working papers defines the role) has distinct advantages over that of principal-as-boss. His position does not inherently pit him against people in the school but rather aligns him along with them in their own endeavors. Of course, there are still the school lunches to contend with, but Damon can expect a qualitatively different sort of interaction in the course of his everyday work than that which faces most principals.

The traditional boss-worker dichotomy simply does not describe the state of affairs at McCarthy-Towne, and neither for that matter do most of the traditional descriptions of public school education. Traditional teacher-student relations, traditional teacher-teacher relations, traditional teacher-parent relations, and traditional curricula have all been scrutinized and redesigned by the staff, which also maintains an ongoing involvement in setting and executing school policy. The staff consists of all the full-time employees of the school—classroom teachers, specialists, and aides (there has been serious talk of including custodians) who, together, have run the school in the New England fashion of direct town-meeting democracy.

The educational fare they have devised is of a special order, a sort of second generation of open education. They have labeled themselves an "alternative school," and do constitute a real alternative to the other elementary schools in the Acton system from which parents may choose to send their children. They also distinguish themselves from other experiments in alternative schooling. In a working paper they reject "the image of this school as a do-your-own-thing school." They say that they want teachers to be humanists and their humanism is not of the "all is groovy" variety—they are savvy enough to take a stand against "habitual teacher praise of students" because of their belief that such praise inhibits real growth in the long run. In addition, one goal of the school at its inception which has continued unwaveringly in its history has been the pursuit of high academic achievement by students. McCarthy-Towne students have always done at least as well on standardized tests as the students in other schools in the system.

Much of the thrust of the school's educational work rests on the staff's expressed belief that children are people, and consequently are in a position to assume some sort of control over what they are to learn. The staff has worked extensively with the educator Caleb Cattegno, who advocates placing "teaching subordinate to learning"—that is carrying out teaching in such a way as to guide a learner rather than to mentally shape him or her to fit a pre-existing mold. A status report prepared by the staff refers to children as "people in process" who deserve respect, and teachers as people "who are comfortable with providing the structure and authority of learning situations as well as the flexibility and opportunity for humor, calm, and activity, all of which are necessary to free the child to be at peace with what he needs to learn and do." Students are guided to assume responsibility for themselves in the course of their own educational development, encouraged and helped instead of being led by the noses. The message is reinforced in more subjective areas, too, even encompassing everyday classroom processes like lining up. Children do not line up and get dismissed to their buses at the end of the school day; instead, they sit and chat informally, listening for the public address system to announce their bus. Even the first-graders are never told when to go, and there are very few students who forget, probably fewer than those lost in the traditional game of line up.

Actual classroom activity seems even to exceed these expectations, as teachers really do refrain from arbitrary authority in favor of talking things out. In fact, "talking things out" seems to be one approach the staff draws on frequently in treating children as people. Two boys I saw engaged in the sort of brawl marked by both a mad flurry of activity and a total absence of injury were not separated by an onlooking teacher except so that they could sit down and "talk it out" (which they—calmly—did).

Normal classroom activity highlights busy, quiet, individual work, comprised largely of students' drawing from the wealth of imaginative resources in the classrooms and following their explorations through on their own. The seriousness with which they approach this exploration shows through from the very moment they enter the classrooms, when they hang up their coats and walk immediately to the files to pick up their corrected, notated work to look over and follow up on—and these were the first graders. The older students carry on similarly, pursuing their own endeavors and brushing up on what they've gone over within class groups that the teachers convene for specific subjects.

Still more notable than the school's philosophy and its apparent success in sticking with it is their ability to do it with creativity, imagination, and a sense of humanity. Everything is an educational resource. When I visited in mid-spring, even the unwitting maple trees surrounding the school had been pulled into the educational process, with spigots driven into their sides and buckets to collect sap as part of some class' science-social living unit. Children moved about inside the classrooms and hallways without the burden of teacher oppression to hunch their shoulders. It was less like the elementary schools with which I am familiar and more like a community of peers. All this is not to suggest that the school is free of problems in its philosophy of education or in its delivery of that philosophy (in fact, the problems are numerous and, some say, serious), but rather to point out that the school *has* a philosophy and that the philosophy is a product of the collective input of its staff. (Some staff meetings are given over only to a discussion of the philosophy of their pedagogy.) The mere existence of a pedagogic philosophy in a public elementary school is not to be overlooked. Some attempt at a uniform philosophy presents children with a very different sort of social environment than that which they would encounter in an "every teacher a sovereign" arrangement.

My friend Aaron Fleisher makes the critical comment about higher education that "so few professors around here have anything to profess." Something to profess in teaching entails a level of personal input and thought of a qualitatively different sort than that of grinding out the lessons. For an individual teacher, having something to profess marks a difference between mere production and craftsmanship.

Beyond the existence of the philosophy, its emphasis on community is also important for the school because it is in a community where people interrelate as people rather than objects. Students are people with rights and responsibilities. Parents are also people, incorporated into the program of the school to a remarkable extent as volunteers in a wide range of activities in and outside classrooms. Parents are not seen as teachers' enemies, but rather more as colleagues in the joint enterprise of the school. Parents were instrumental in the original organization of the school, working with the core group of teachers. Continued parent involvement is an expectation in the school, formalized by a commitment of staff time to organize parent volunteers.

Perhaps it is the community aspect of McCarthy-Towne that is most important, the aspect that assumes that teachers will drop in on each other during the course of a day and comment on, even criticize, what they see and live to tell about it. How much more typical it is in schools for teachers to regard their classrooms as holy ground to be defended against marauding supervisors and leering, so-called colleagues. Ignoring this Maginot Line at the classroom door, teachers are able to provide a very needed kind of psychological support and to learn from the insights of others. The staff that upholds the humanity of its students also seeks to be viewed as people with interests and foibles of their own, in and outside the classroom.

The staff is a friendly group, not devoid of the jealousies and neuroses that may exist in any group (indeed some say they have more than a usual proportion of these) but uniquely determined to work through their conflicts, to "talk it out." They have more than a usual degree of motivation to talk things out because in running the school, most "things" are their things. Many of the usual teacher gripes—the curriculum a teacher may be forced to work with, the hiring and firing of colleagues, the tone of humor and authority in the school—are within the normal jurisdiction of staff policymaking. There are still some decisions presided over by the town and the state, but the staff's control of McCarthy-Towne has significantly widened the input a teacher can have on his or her work environment. As in an experiment in job redesign, workers' control over their work is extended, and a broader range of involvement and more general use of knowledge is possible.

The importance of such input for teachers became apparent at a meeting in which room assignments were discussed. Teachers were concerned with what room they would be in because different rooms had different physical features that they perceived as interesting, helpful, or detrimental, and the teachers wanted to sort it out so that, generally, people got what they wanted. During the discussion, it also came out that room assignments established a social environment as well as a physical one, and teachers wanted to be sure that people clustered together by the physical layout were also interested in working together. Then there was the issue of being forced to work together: some teachers preferred relative isolation, some wanted to be in a "team" setup. One of them wondered, "Can we get a computer dating service to help us work this out?"

Everyone expressed some strong preferences about room assignments, making it abundantly clear that the assignments would affect their teaching. The complexity of the discussion made clear also that no one of the teachers could have spoken for all of them and that they all needed some kind of input (even simple veto power would be helpful) to ensure that all the teachers were satisfied. Moreover, the discussion surfaced some new ways of thinking about room assignments that caused a few people to rethink their individual ideas. The end result was a real group product, more complex than any individual could have constructed.

The existence of such a school in a public system is, to put it mildly, an anomaly. McCarthy-Towne happened in Acton mostly because the system wanted an "open" school. As the drive for the open school progressed, a core of parents and teachers evolved to speak most forcefully on its behalf. No complementary force existed on the side of the system and the group found itself in a position to call the shots, which it shortly learned to do with some proficiency. As the idea of the school progressed, it became increasingly "natural" for the teacher-management structure to hold sway.

Finally, in the year before the school was opened, all
the teachers in the system were invited and the core
who applied took over the remainder of the hiring.

Personnel has always been a big issue in the school,
consuming much of the time and energy of the initial
core. The new venture would depend largely on the
people who got it off the ground, especially as the venture was to be actually run by them. Each interview
for a teacher was then, in a sense, also an interview for
a principal and vice principal. In addition, candidates
needed to be screened carefully for interpersonal as
well as pedagogic skills because the participatory
management of the school depended on their ability
both to listen and to "talk things through."

At the outset everyone participated in interviewing
new staff, but the number of people that grew to be
involved began to make the interview oppressive for
the candidates and the amount of time nearly all-
consuming. Committees were then chosen in the various
grade-level groupings to bring recommendations back
to the whole group for a final decision. Eventually and
on schedule, the school acquired a very competent and
dedicated staff from the abundant pool of candidates
offered by the New England region's especially concentrated version of the teacher surplus.

The excitement and vitality of initiation, novelty,
and growth helped carry the school through its initial
years, but the kinds of demands the school was making
on staff grew to be perceived as excessive. Staff members put an enormous amount of time and involvement
into the school. The staff's meetings and group process
rapidly took on the trappings of "process-meeting angst"
so familiar to members of other collectives and food
co-ops. Meetings were long and involved, and it seemed
that any form of human contact was intense. Like the

mainstays in a co-op, the original core of McCarthy-Towne staff began to "burn out," but they have gone about attempting to reduce the flame instead of helping to extinguish it: rather than leaving, they have begun to attempt to change the school to enable it to continue but on a reduced, more efficient level of their involvement. They will not relinquish their ties with the organization, but they are also very mindful of its original participatory form. They know what bureaucratization is, and they don't want it. What they do want is the best of both—a school the staff can run without it running them.

It is possible to see this effort to relinquish involvement as simple, inevitable fleeing from an arrangement that was unrealistic all along, an arrangement that was the original quirk output of a small group of fanatics with unlimited time on their hands. Perhaps the whole idea of teacher management of a school is unworkable except in circumstances where teachers do nothing else but work on the school. However, it is also possible to view the changing organization as a foray into organizational learning—that is, the school's acquiring the ability to satisfy its members' changing needs. In this case, the issue is not dead but vital to incorporating a current diversity of kinds of involvement—some staffers still want to pour their lives into the school while some want mostly out. The issue here seems mostly technical—learning how to make the school jump through a different and more complex set of hoops.

The transition the staff is attempting to make is from direct democracy (in which everyone has direct involvement in running things) to participatory, representative democracy (where influence is indirect, through elected representatives and committees). They feel they have too much involvement in management and want to give up some of it, and yet retain both some form of indirect input and leave open the option for renewing direct involvement.

An Organizational Development Committee of the staff pieced together a proposal outlining an overlapping structure of small groups, individuals, and committees which it assigned specific tasks and levels of responsibilities. A chart outlining the structure (see appendix) details these assignments and begins to affirm the possibility that a representative form may be feasible. The problem with implementing it is one of irony in that the new form will require some initial energy before it will work well, and it is the very dwindling of energy that has brought the form about. It seems inevitable that the design and implementation of such a transition will occur late, as the form will not be conceived until it is needed.

There does seem to be more than enough of a residual commitment to the participatory form at McCarthy-Towne to carry the organization development proposal from staff and parents, but this may be one of the least serious problems the school faces. Dwindling enrollments in the system, a product of the town's (for that matter, the nation's) dwindling birth rate, are imposing serious pressures on the school from within and without. Personnel decisions made by the staff are now more of the "who among us will go?" variety as the school strives to function within its budget. Placing personnel cuts within the purview of the personnel themselves has spawned a questioning for many teachers of their own career paths as they have sought to keep the school viable. New kinds of part-time arrangements and rotating leaves of absence are under discussion. Most important, the topic of cuts, though difficult, does not hold the aura of malicious intrigue that prevails in traditionally organized schools facing the same problem.

Besides the direct issue of personnel cuts, the reduced birth rate has had the more general effect of creating an economy of scarcity within the system, allowing less leeway for activities that are not immediately effective and efficient. Any kind of exploration is a luxury whose costs become increasingly prohibitive as there are fewer resources for expeditions.

Yet the survival of McCarthy-Towne in a recognizable variant of its current form seems a certainty, for there are too many people with too much emotion and intelligence invested for it to be any other way. (A chart outlining the structure of McCarthy-Towne in an appendix to this book provides more details and explores, along with the chart of Open Design, the uses of such charts.)

COLLECTIVES OF PROFESSIONALS

McCarthy-Towne, Wilson & Burnstein, the individual planning consultant, and Open Design each expand the horizons of their respective professions along lines that make sense both for their members and for the professions themselves. Each has confronted some of the basic issues taken for granted in their respective professions (relationships between professionals and clients; relationships among professionals; basic work processes like working drawings, the need for an office, the use of a secretary, the divisions of work) and reshaped them in ways that either produce more economically sensible or more humanly satisfying results.

The groups stand both on their ability to satisfy members' interests better than more traditional forms of practice and on their ability to meet baseline requirements of their respective professions for production and organizational viability. Traditional firms trying

to emulate some aspects of these collective arrangements have their hearts in the right place but are essentially misguided, because what "makes" all of these
arrangements is their wholeness, their continuity, their
indigenous rooting in their members. No one can give
it as a gift, because it belongs to everyone.

CHAPTER FOUR

Minding
Their Business

In a sense, all the work arrangements described in
this book, including crafts and professions, are businesses. This chapter will pay specific attention to the
financial and legal aspects of various work arrangements
and to a number of groups that might fit the category
of small businesses: retail establishments, restaurants,
and an insurance company.

Thinking about the work groups as businesses helps
identify some of the problems they are likely to encounter, and the conventional wisdom holds that the
number and seriousness of such problems are alarming.
Senator Gaylord Nelson, chairman of the Senate Small
Business Committee, believes "our small businesses are
sinking deeper into a morass of Federal rules, regula-
tions and paper work. They are victimized by discrim-
inatory Federal income tax laws. They are being driven
out of business by confiscatory estate taxes."[1]

Changing Times, the Kiplinger Magazine, warns
potential starters of small businesses of the disadvan-
tages of getting started at this time: business failures
are up, indicating tough times in general and stiff
competition for the survivors; inflation has made
shoppers more conservative in many aspects of buying.[2]

Still, *Changing Times* advances the argument that overall, things are not so bad and even if they were, "real" entrepreneurs with "viable" businesses needn't hold back.

What seems to be the downfall of most business failures (90 percent, as analyzed by Dun and Bradstreet[3]) is a lack of managerial experience, which *Changing Times* specifies as marketing know-how, product knowledge, accounting skills, personnel activities, and vast reserves of personal energy. Lack of adequate capital or initial funding also cuts short many business starts. *Changing Times* recommends having enough capital not only to open, but to cover operating costs for three to four months. Businesses that succumb to these and other problems contribute to small business's high rate of failure: only about one-third survive beyond five years, and about a third don't survive beyond one year.

To help people through this dangerous jungle, *Changing Times* offers financial guidesheets and refers to the information resources offered by the government's Small Business Administration, which include numerous publications, seminars, some individual counseling, and a few loans. The IRS also doles out helpful information, and a publication called *Small Business Reporter* is interesting. *Changing Times* warns that it may be difficult to pry information from existing businesses that may feel threatened by upstarts, but the possibility of getting real information makes it worth the effort. Besides, businesses of the kind described in this book are usually very helpful in giving whatever advice they can. In addition, the Vocations for Social Change offices in various cities can be very helpful.

The best kind of information, however, is provided by experience, and people can acquire that in a variety of ways. Craftspeople often gain experience by beginning with a part-time endeavor. This allows them to develop their skills while limiting risks. Some members of work co-ops do a stint in traditional versions of the work, and some do a form of apprenticeship.

The nuts and bolts of small businesses will be described (as they were in other chapters) in the contexts of descriptions of specific enterprises: an insurance company, an inn, a record store, a plant store, a restaurant, and, to begin, a woodworking collective.

THE NEW HAMBURGER CABINET WORKS

The way things are arranged, members of New Hamburger have to walk too far in the warehouse space to get to the wood supply. This isn't completely bad since walking breaks up the work and gives people a chance to look in on the several other groups who share the space. Still, the group is coming to feel that they can talk whenever they want to and they don't like being inconvenienced when they want to get at the wood. The six members of the group who are working (a few others are on jobs in the field, doing light contracting or custom work at a site; a few others are simply unaccounted for) bring up the woodrack topic at lunch when the shop is relatively quiet, the buzzing, humming, and sometimes screaming machines shut off while all four groups on the floor eat their lunch.

Members of the group sit on sawdust-covered benches during the lunch break, passing around several containers of Chinese food picked up at a local restaurant. The first issues that they discuss have to do with where a rack could go. The six of them (four men and two women that day) consider what one would expect to come up in any woodworking shop, collective or not: what other items will have to be moved to accommodate the rack, where the most convenient location would be, how any location might be susceptible to theft. The group's "tool-lord," who is more influential than any landlord, is concerned about how the rack will simplify the task of accounting for loose tools.

They also review some more personal concerns, and these get as much if not more attention than efficiency issues. For example, one potential location is ruled out because it would involve removing a wall that the collective recently worked hard to build. Another is vetoed because it would limit access to the bathroom, another because it would protrude into the group's workspace in a way people think would be uncomfortable.

Then there's the whole matter of where the woodrack should come from. There seems to be unanimous agreement that the collective doesn't want to make it from scratch themselves, but people aren't very enthusiastic about getting one that's completely assembled, either. A metal pipe fabricating shop nearby emerges as a possible solution, and the discussion begins to center on whether to use plain or fancy pipe.

As the other shops on the floor end their lunch break, they switch on planers, joiners, saws, and drills that render further discussion impossible for New Hamburger. The group has made some headway, though, settling on a place to shop for the rack and narrowing the possible locations to two or three out of the original dozen. They clean up the lunch packaging and head back to their work.

Work for that day consists of three projects to which people gravitate, except for one person who leaves to bid on some outside carpentry work and another who moves into the group's tiny office to catch up on some bookkeeping. One woman returns to a table top she had glued together before lunch, checking the tension on the massive metal clamps bonding the planked top together. Two of the men return to some sawing for a project not then far enough along to be distinguishable. The other woman returns to a wooden assemblage that occupied the central floorspace of the group's work area. Seven feet long, several feet high, and several feet deep, its wooden skeleton still clamped together pending the drying of its glued joints, the assemblage could have been a very tall closet on its side, a desk with built-in bookshelves, or wood sculpture. The woman working on it says it is a kitchen cabinet, though, and the form became much more comprehensible.

The group does not work as a group on most projects, but divides work according to a constantly changing mix of efficiency and whim. Hadley, one of the group, explains, "We *could* work together on anything, but we usually do projects as individuals when the projects are small, we're working for a friend, or someone in the group is interested in the kind of work the job requires." Working absolutely alone when surrounded by close friends is an impossibility, though, and everyone in the collective agreed that there is a lot of kibitzing and cross-criticism about everybody's work, "especially behind their backs," one member teases. The group unanimously agrees that they do not hesitate to criticize work that they feel is of poor quality; they simply don't want inferior work to carry their name.

Workmanship-craftsmanship mixed with autonomy and independence rank as the group's raison d'être, displacing other possible motivations, like a desire to get rich. People in the group make four to five thousand dollars a year but claim they could earn much more if they chose to. As it is, they choose to work more for the sake of the work itself. "We work twice as hard as people in an ordinary shop," one person notes, "but then, we take a lot more time off. When we work we put in long hours and get very involved with the project. When we finish, we'll often just take off for a few days, maybe even a week, to rest, and maybe get involved with something else at home. When we say we work here full-time, that includes days off when we want them and lots of time for diddling around.

"It's up to people's discretion to take the time off and work as much as seems right. We work on an hourly basis, and a portion of what we earn goes back to the shop to pay the rent. Profit, if there is any, is also redistributed proportionately according to hours worked." (Members of the group overhearing this explanation broke into simultaneous applause at the word "proportionately.")

Group members limit their income not only by being self-indulgent in their use of time off but also in their choice of work. A woman explained how the group decided long ago not to get involved with stock lines of furniture, items of relatively high profit, because they would make the work uninteresting. The group would have to make sure that its inventory was always under control, and they would spend more time cranking the pieces out and less in design. Other groups have taken the stock item approach and become (in certain limited circles, anyway) relatively wealthy and famous.

New Hamburger has shunned the stock item approach because it makes the work very boring. It requires a system for making the pieces, so the group must direct its energy away from design of the furniture to design of assembly-line process. New Hamburger had recently completed an order of twenty large cabinets for a university near its Cambridge, Massachusetts, workspace and had not quite recovered from the order's impact. "I thought it would never end," one of the women laments. "We just kept making the same cuts, gluing the same joints—it was awful. I was ecstatic to see the last of those things leave the shop, and by the time it did I had no feeling at all for the money we made on the things." Other members affirm that their experience with the cabinets removed any lingering notions they may have had about exploring stock items.

In the approach New Hamburger has taken to custom work, members design a piece with input from the client and from other members. Members follow each piece of work through from beginning to end, often even doing their own purchasing of materials and their own book-keeping. The group relies on referrals and word-of-mouth advertising. Newspaper and display ads are both too expensive and "too commercial." Overall, concentrating on custom work sets going a system that influences the work setting, beginning with adver-tising and image and reaching out into the process of how the work gets done.

Custom work sets a tone that enables the group to keep their own interests in the work as a first priority. Customers are viewed as patrons of the arts. "When somebody walks in the door, you can't necessarily talk them into wanting what you want to make," Hadley explains. "You have a pretty good chance, but some-times you have to make what they want, and to that extent there's a compromise. Still, that's nothing like producing it en masse, plugging it together, and hoping that it makes it to the store in one piece."

The desire to do woodworking in the most interesting way possible traces from the group's current stress on custom work back to their founding six years ago when "one of the motivations for starting was that we wanted to do the kind of work we wanted to do." The three original members balanced their desire with a desire for free time. "Most of us have kids and we wanted time beyond the forty-hour work week." Then as now, people viewed the group as a vehicle, a way to enable them to earn a living that did not exist among available traditional job offerings.

The group also simply provided a job in times when work was very scarce. A few members had tried to get traditional woodworking jobs but encountered a catch 22 in arrangements with unions. One person recalls the applications he made at cabinetmaking shops: "They'd say, 'If you're a member of the union, we'll maybe let you have a job here.' So then I'd go to the union and they'd say, 'If you get a job, maybe we'll let you join the union.'"

Looking back, current members agree that the group's founding did not hinge on collective frustration and dauntlessness, however intrepid people were, but on coming up with the necessary capital and finding a potential group member who had a well-stocked supply of tools. "Without that one person who had the tools and most of the money, I don't think any individual here could have done it," one member contends. The tools were an expensive factor, as group members showed off some recent acquisitions of clamps, items that can cost fifty dollars each and get used by the group in its more active moments in sets of more than a dozen.

Citing a book he is reading on "the laws of money," one member observes, "One of the laws of money is 'do it.' You can always wait for a better time, but you may never get anything done. The main thing is to have the idea and to do it; the rest will follow." The group has shied away from taking out bank loans, relying instead on personal loans, bothering friends, and scrounging when they needed capital. No one is enthusiastic about the topic of government or foundation aid to small businesses; they feel that anybody who really wants to could make a go of things and that aid programs would not affect the eventual outcome and success of any business. The key, they feel, is in putting together the right people and looking long and hard enough for the right situation.

They also feel that today's right situation might turn into tomorrow's boondoggle, though, and describe their growth and development from a "tentative" beginning to the dawning realization that, "Hey, this is working." They are unable to recall how the original group decided on the name "New Hamburger," but one woman remembers that "Wooden Plenty" was a close contender. They took on and dropped members during their six years, though they noted that the only people who left entirely were folks who moved out of the area.

Their recent move from a Roxbury warehouse to the Cambridge location enabled them to make the whole operation more efficient. "It was a little traumatic, moving from a place after we had finally gotten ends to meet," Hadley remarks. "We had forgotten how much of a problem the old building was. For one thing, the elevator kept catching on fire. You couldn't ride it: you'd put some materials on it, then run downstairs to catch them."

The rent in the Cambridge place is a bit higher but the layout allows them to be more productive and makes working more enjoyable. It's cleaner and brighter, and sharing the building with other co-ops makes the work situation more interesting. "Technically, all the shops are in competition, but it doesn't work out that way," a member explains. "We each have our own kinds of customers and work specialties. If they really wanted to, customers could get an estimate from us, then walk across the floor and get a competing price from Walrus or the other groups. In practice, it doesn't happen." The shops share tools and expertise as well as rent, and in the beginning met weekly to keep in touch. Now contact is less frequent, relegated to special times for solving problems.

The overall tone of activity at New Hamburger has settled similarly to that of an unusual business engaged, almost in spite of its own disbelief, in business as usual. They've solved the initial problems that cripple so many businesses—working out logistical tangles. With health insurance, for example, the problem for them is not finding where and how to get it (they've located all available sources) but how to pay for it. Rates are high and getting higher, and the group has to pay its own way. Still, this sort of problem is of a much different order than operating in a vacuum of uncertainty. At this point, after six years, New Hamburger is not likely to be plagued by many surprises.

Building on the comings and goings of a workforce that demands variety and interesting work taken at their own pace, New Hamburger has evolved into an organization that matches economic viability with individual satisfaction. With custom work in demand, the woodworking market currently has room to allow such a group to function. The issue now is refinement and improvement in productivity and satisfying members' interests. Sometimes these overlap to satisfy both, as reflected in the decision-making about the woodrack. As long as they can afford it, the group will continue to decide on the basis of what people want than what money dictates. In fact, as it is currently defined, the group may never be able to afford to make its decisions on any other grounds. When money matters come to reign, the group will begin to look like a traditional shop and the sense of the thing will be lost.

Now the group is not merely a well-oiled machine

for producing woodwork and cabinetry but an artists' enclave and, perhaps most important, a group for its own sake. On the same agenda with the woodrack decision is an issue to which the group gives equal if not greater attention: should they buy tickets to the mailmen's ball? If they don't, would they be doomed to a future devoid of incoming mail? And if they do buy the tickets, should they surprise the mailman and actually go to the thing, and maybe bring forty or fifty friends?

New Hamburger is representative of other collective work arrangements in a number of ways, but other kinds of groups also deserve some attention. International Group Plans is at the "big" end of things; it at once embodies the awesome potential of self-management and the inevitable problems of depersonalization and logistical balancing that are a part of "going big."

INTERNATIONAL GROUP PLANS

"It's all a hype," confides an executive at the Washington, D.C., offices of the worker-run insurance company International Group Plans. "People are self-managed here only in those areas in which no one higher up wants to accept responsibility. Self-management is not a bad concept, but it's being done badly here. For us, it's mostly all responsibilities but no rights." He talks in a low voice, smoking a cigarette nervously and casting furtive glances over his shoulder. He planned to leave within a few months, he says, but he has not yet announced the decision formally and wants to keep it a secret until he feels it necessary to "go public."

One malcontent out of the 350 employees at IGP would not be a bad track record even for utopia, but it's very difficult to separate fact from feeling and fiction in the plush offices amid files, computers, office machinery, and people. It would certainly be a serious mistake to dismiss IGP out of hand as someone's office commune gone awry. Its sheer size, financial success, and over- all volume of human effort distinguish it and the issues for which it stands. It has been described in articles and books, and received the scrutiny of a Bill Moyers telecast on public television. It seems very successful in much of what it attempts, but there are also some bothersome paradoxes, even beyond what one might expect to hear from an employee who has chosen to leave.

One fairly pleasant paradox is the business atmos- phere of IGP, which attempts to mix some feeling for humanity with less sensitive, traditional business norms. Employees can and do wear pretty much whatever they want to, though those who interact with the "outside world" are urged to conform in dress to facilitate com- munication when they go to meetings. Those who work in the office appear in anything from farmers' overalls to short shorts. The sight of an executive in overalls is not easily forgotten, and it sets the pace for the rest of the company. One clerk speaks with pride of "workers in other offices in the building (Rand occupies some space there) who don't know what to think of IGP people; they seem to look on us as waifs."

There's a small waiting area for visitors and clients outside the working office. It features the obligatory arrangement of office furniture, business magazines, plush carpeting, and a receptionist enclosed behind a sliding glass panel. In the days when many clients came to the office, the office legend is that they were often kept waiting during the scramble inside the office to find someone who looked presentable.

The seriousness with which people approach their

work in this atmosphere of apparent leisure is another
pleasant paradox, because it does in fact appear to be
possible for people to be productive while wearing
jeans. Indeed, the work takes precedence over most
traditional business rituals. A vice-president notes,
"It's very difficult to keep people interested; some of
the work simply is not all that challenging. We try
and make it as easy as possible to get the work done,
and sometimes that means scrapping traditional ideas
like dress codes. We work in the various departments
with production standards that are pretty typical in
this business, maybe even a little higher, and as long
as people meet those, we don't make many other demands. Also, we try to make other kinds of opportunities available to employees that take into account the
dullness of some of the work."

Some of these opportunities are for leadership—
workers may become team leaders of their work areas.
Other opportunities exist in areas outside immediate
work, in tasks of various committees. Benefits and
wages comprise another kind of opportunity, and IGP
is noteworthy for its comprehensive benefits package.
Wages are about at the market median.

More important than the lax dress code, some other
aspects of IGP that follow from a focus on getting the
work done include flexible hours and scheduling. Work
teams of a half-dozen or so employees set their hours
around the demand of the work. This aspect of the
company's organization has made it particularly appealing for working parents who need to be able to juggle
their work hours.

Flexible hours and scheduling, and a lax dress code
bespeak a respect for people as well as a focus on the
work—other approaches to a focus on work have usually been noteworthy for their disregard of people.

Respect at IGP surfaces in a number of other ways too, such as the screening of job candidates by workers themselves in their own departments. Workers also elect their own team leaders or supervisors.

All this concern for workers would in itself be noteworthy, but it is only a part of what IGP attempts. The other, more complicated aspect of IGP is its self-management, and it is this that underlies the humane work environment. It is in self-management, however, that the paradoxes of IGP become more troublesome, beginning perhaps with the notion of self-management itself and its origins in the company. The logistics of self-determination in a community of 350 are staggering —how can so many organize at all?

The logistical problems of organization for self-management are compounded at IGP by the fact that nearly all the employees did not come to IGP because of its self-management; in fact, most of them did not even know about it. Most apparently come to work at IGP because of the working conditions and benefits and thus are unprepared for the commitments necessary for self-management to become a reality. There are many opportunities for involvement at a variety of levels ranging from small-group task organization and scheduling to policy setting in the Community Relations Assembly (CRA), a body that resembles a New England town meeting. Employees easily become involved in matters closely related to their work, but the reasoning behind involvement becomes less clear in most abstract areas. Nonetheless, it is precisely in the more abstract policy areas that real self-management can begin to distinguish itself from more basic humanized work. Recently a series of classes was instituted to help people understand the company and participate more.

CRA members are elected by workers from the different departments and include a range of seniority and rank. The weekly meetings of the CRA usually draw about fifteen people, with more attending for an important issue publicized in advance. The CRA contributed to a legal defense fund and toward support of a neighborhood halfway house. Currently they are working on refining the rules for cost-of-living increases, sabbaticals, and severance pay. The purview of the CRA is policy-making, and it approaches its work seriously.

Perhaps the most paradoxical aspect of self-management at IGP is that represented by a paradoxical person, Jim Gibbons, IGP's founder. Employees' characterizations of Gibbons range from "philosopher-king" to "benevolent despot" to "supersalesman" to "egomaniac." Some employees single him out as responsible for all the company's problems while others believe any of the company's success must be attributed directly to him. An older woman who was a team leader (a section supervisor of a half-dozen others) in Claims swore that if he ever went, she would not stay either.

Gibbons built the company, beginning about five years ago on the strength of his sales and administrative capabilities, and the source of current debate is whether, and how, his involvement continues. According to employees, he does not manage but rather pursues work in sales, his specialty. However, some people believe that his influence continues to be strongly felt. The worker who was about to resign contends, "Either we agree with him or we go back to punching clocks." The image of Gibbons that emerges in all this is as a sort of latter-day Robert Owen, striving single-handedly, and very competently, to establish a self-managed organization; and this is the essence of the paradox—one person establishing self-management.

The task makes demands that may be impossible to meet perfectly, and it may well be that there is no need to do so. IGP's paradoxes may be catalysts for discussion and articulation of problems. In any case, the one person-founder structure of IGP engenders characteristic organizational problems of socialization and education quite different from those seen in smaller, "organic" groups, and Gibbons, for all the controversy, could never be accused of being boring or insincere.

But there are yet more paradoxes, even beyond Jim Gibbons, and perhaps one of the most complicated of them is the ownership of the company.

Employees own half of it, and clients own the other half. It's a kind of mix of classic profit sharing with the brilliant selling point for the large associations that comprise the bulk of the company's business that they not only buy insurance, but own part of the insurance company.

Ownership of the company means a lot to employees when they can "cash in their chips" and take their share of the value that the company's stock has appreciated. All employees get the same amount, regardless of rank in the company—about $3,600 for a worker who had been there two years. However lucrative, the meaning of the ownership plan to workers is limited by its abstraction. They can benefit from it only when they leave, when they collect profits on the shares. The actual shares are held in trust.

Even when self-ownership is salient it can cause problems. As one clerk pointed out, it may sometimes conflict with self-management. The interests of owners clash with the interests of workers, especially when the concerns of the latter are more immediately felt. In a sense, every decision of self-management also affects self-ownership, but understandably it may be

difficult for workers to relate their desire for longer
vacations to an anticipated reduction in their profit-
sharing.

And then there are the clients, most of whom are not
at all likely bedfellows in ownership with IGP's workforce. In fact, many of the associations with whom
IGP deals are related in one way or another to the military. Associations of retired officers and military
reservists like to offer their members whatever services
might be helpful to them as a way of providing service
and building their own organization. IGP sells insurance (actually IGP is not an insurance company, but
an agent for another company) at reduced rates to the
members of such organizations through direct mail
solicitation. Members get low-cost insurance, the
associations get an improved relationship with their
members and part ownership in IGP, and IGP gets vast
amounts of business. Presently it services nearly half
a million subscribers.

While the office environment at IGP works itself into
a state of internal mellowness, then, workers must deal
frequently with clients (co-owners, no less) whose military background may raise a considerable amount of
discomfort. In addition to the general conceptual difficulties of dealing with military people, there are also
some specific events that bother workers. "They call
to ask for some information," one clerk says, "but they
don't ask—they order. They think everybody is a
sergeant."

Client choice and marketing have not yet come under
the influence of the CRA, and they are indicative of the
inherent problems of self-management in a large company because they underscore the need for a decentrali-
zation of knowledge that could well consume most of
the workers' time. Classic Greek democracy was based

on a widely shared understanding of the system which even necessitated education to help make citizens conversant with the issues. The issues at IGP, however, may require a level of understanding that few can attain; marketing techniques, for example, may never get discussed in a helpful way unless everyone goes to school for three or four years to learn them.

Here is a fairly close incarnation of sociologist Robert Michel's Iron Law of Oligarchy—the specialized knowledge of some workers translates easily, perhaps even inevitably, into power. Here also, however, is a credible attempt to smash the oligarchy in the form of the CRA, whose inquiry is unrestricted (if not conclusive) and rooted in a broad representation of the whole group of workers. They may not be able to eliminate the intrinsic power of those with specialized knowledge but they at least can minimize it by keeping it under the continuing scrutiny of open dialogue and debate.

Much of what self-management is about seems to hinge, then, on how people treat knowledge, even more so than on which of them has it. In a truly self-managed firm, it might not be necessary for everyone to possess the same knowledge as everyone else, but rather to make that knowledge accessible. Norms would need to exist that validate the inquiry of those who seek to know and sanction against mystification. One way to accomplish this very effectively is informally, in the ways in which people interact, and here IGP seems headed in the right direction. The implicit pervasive message that "we are all people here" must be an important underpinning of open dialogue. To support the informal norms of inquiry and interaction, formal access to knowledge via organized classes can also be helpful, and here again IGP has made some inroads by making various classes in company business available to workers.

The norms of communication create yet another paradox for workers, though, as two employees described their interpretations. One woman, impressed by the attempts at communication, remarks, "They're always trying to keep you informed around here—newsletters, flyers, notices are always coming out, and they really let you know what's going on in the whole company." The resignee-to-be, however, sees the attempts at communication differently: "Self-management is the excuse that lots of people around here use to stick their noses into other peoples' business. Sometimes, with everybody watching out for everybody else it gets to be like a soap opera or worse."

In this sense, IGP is not much different from any of the smaller, more marginal work collectives (a number of which, like the Third Day Plant Store and the Collective Impressions Print Shop, are located within easy walking distance) that all seem to generate veritable beehives of soap opera activities in addition to whatever their primary products are supposed to be. But there are some crucial differences between the other groups and IGP, extending well beyond the immediately discernible difference in size and focusing mostly on assumptions, expectations, and the nature of work.

IGP begins with the assumption that the work of the business is essentially boring. It generally leaves that assumption unchallenged or even strengthens it by developing employee benefits external to the work. People have generally not come together beneath the IGP umbrella to refine their pursuit of excellence and joy in the insurance business, but rather to do whatever must be done to earn a living. The basic tenets of doing business have thus far gone unquestioned even though there is much in the very nature of the insurance business that invites questioning. As one of the clerks put it, "Insurance is not exactly a utilitarian business."

IGP is a company, not an insurance commune, and as such it likely will not exercise as much flexibility as a smaller group. A recent *New Yorker* cartoon depicts a man addressing a board of directors meeting, with the caption: "We could streamline the organization, or step up our advertising, or issue new stock. But since it's such a lovely day, why don't we just go out of business?"[4]

The option of calling it quits or of undertaking a radically different approach to the business does not seem to be in the cards for IGP, even if the CRA develops muscle well beyond the most optimistic current predictions. The size of the company and the spectre of a philosopher-king will further limit how far things can go.

While IGP is not of the same order as the collectives that enshrine work and fine-tune group process, it is also a far cry from the other insurance companies on the block. The purists can justifiably criticize it, but IGP has undeniably devised a way of doing business in insurance that differs significantly from the norm. In the business world the norms are more like universals, so any deviation is significant. IGP is especially so because of its financial strength and the comprehensive way in which it is assembled. The pieces for real self-management are all there; they work together fairly well now, and even without attaining perfection IGP is a remarkable phenomenon.

In contrast with the size of IGP and the nature of insurance business, a small New England inn offers another example of self-designed work.

THE TAMWORTH INN

It's difficult to imagine Bill and Susan McCarthy as anything but innkeepers. They have a way of welcom-

ing guests, cooking, tending bar, and doing all the
things that go into keeping an inn that bears ready
witness to Bill's view that "Running this inn is sort
of like always having house guests, and keeping a
party going." The inn is decorated in a classic old
New England style befitting its respectable centennial-
plus age, neither sparse nor ostentatious but cozy,
modest, and comfortable, and with great sensitivity
to its age. It divides the "business district" of Tamworth, New Hampshire, from the rolling fields that
eventually become the White Mountains. It's a postcard inn in a postcard town. "Business district" seems
an awkward misnomer for the tidy cluster of houses, a
church, a few stores, and a summer theater. Unlike
some hostelries, the inn is an integral part of the town:
townspeople come over for a drink when square dances
are held in the hall next door, and throughout the year.
Members of the Barnstormers' summer theater, one of
the town's major industries, stay at the inn and help
raise the level of summer business to a fever pitch.

The town's tranquility makes itself felt in the inn, in
the paneled bar and dining room, and upstairs in the
lodging. Bill assures me that such is not always the
case, that the current picture of smooth operations
belies the extremely turbulent beginnings of their take-
over a few years ago. "We got here on May 27," he
recalls, "and took over on June 1, right before the summer rush. Our arrival was followed shortly by the
great floods, including a fairly serious threat from the
seemingly innocent creek behind the inn. Then after
the floods came the meat shortage, and then after we
somehow made it through the summer, came gas shortages in the winter.

"Things were so bad at that point we had to turn to
the SBA (Small Business Administration) for a low-

interest loan. They helped bail a lot of us out. Bankruptcy was a live topic then for lots of businesses up here, but in the end, was out of the question—no one would foreclose because there was basically nothing to take." As the various shortages eased up a steady increase in business took hold, and the McCarthys were able to refine their innkeeping skills and work on physical repair. "The place looked like something out of 1935 when we moved in," Bill recalls.

Much of the Tamworth's current success has to be attributed to the McCarthys' adept development of innkeeping skills, the integrated art of a generalist that must involve anything from cooking and small restaurant management to interior decorating and sweeping floors. The skills are not acquired coherently— there is yet no Famous Innkeepers' School, though the idea is probably sound. Nor are the skills hereditary, though one could begin to think so, watching the McCarthys at work in the inn's kitchen, hovering over institutional-size stoves that resemble small metal caverns, winding their way through a forest of hanging pots and vapors rising from the perpetually warming coffee pot.

The McCarthys acquired the skills piecemeal over a number of years, managing a small restaurant, getting involved with antiques, and buying and fixing up small houses. "We did a lot of crazy things," Bill observed. "We never did just one thing. It's not that we were devoid of talent, but that you couldn't quite put it on a sheet of paper."

They had friends in Sandwich, a town near Tamworth, and when they came up (from their home in Pennsylvania) to visit they fell in love with the area. They considered a number of different kinds of businesses, but "Weighing all the factors, an inn seemed most like the right thing for us to do." They sent to state real estate boards in Maine and New Hampshire and turned up four places to examine. "One place in Maine sounded super," Bill remembers, "it had over a hundred acres. But it was hideous, almost scary and desolate. They had these *big* boxes of rat poison, and they were half-eaten.

"We looked at some of the other places and were beginning to think that maybe innkeeping was a bad idea, but then at the end of the day we drove past this place and it looked good. It had its problems all right, but Sue just walked in and started decorating mentally —she could see the potential clearly." They bid on it, but even in buying it there were problems, when negotiations fell through three times. Meanwhile, Bill was leaving his job—an awkward position compounded by the uncertainty of the negotiations.

Flexibility seems to have been an important guiding force for the McCarthys, enabling them to leave Pennsylvania and take on the inn on short notice, and flexibility continues to remain important. After all, the business of innkeeping is based on little that is predictable—the vagaries of weather can pack the house and empty the restaurant cupboards, or leave the inn ghostly, empty, depending. Times of the year also bring cycles, with the business highs of the summer allowing only two or three days off for the season, while winter brings many days off.

The McCarthys ride with the flexibility, and even compound it in some areas, like accounting. "We run a loose ship here. Our accountant is constantly bailing us out," Bill observes. "Our biggest problem is the fundamentals. We could have plenty of money in the bank, and not pay a bill because we had already put it aside."

Flexibility is an indulgence, and the McCarthys often

enjoy it for its own sake. "What innkeeping is really all about," Bill claims, "is living in New Hampshire and taking your family skiing every week." They have also chosen to run the business in a way that emphasizes what is comfortable to them rather than what yields the greatest monetary returns. They only run one advertisement, and in a small country journal, because they rely on word of mouth and believe "you get nicer people that way."

The McCarthys don't seem to have allowed the inn to run their lives, and have recently moved to further ensure the inn's manageability by allowing friends to buy in as partners. Bill has known Doug Conway since their college days, when they worked together in a sub shop, and Doug and his wife Linda had told the McCarthys they might be interested in joining them when they moved to Tamworth. The Conways have bought in as full partners, "the only way" the four felt the arrangement should be handled because of the need for everyone to take some responsibility for every aspect of the inn's operation.

Both the Conways and the McCarthys have children, and the inn business affects family life for them in mixed ways. For the Conways, whose children are young, the inn provides contact with lots of adults and families passing through, but the busiest times demand hiring a babysitter. Sean and Bill (Jr.) McCarthy like the school and have had no trouble making friends. Sue believes the contact they have with people coming to the inn is good for them, and thinks they have about the same kinds of chores and responsibilities as any youths. Overhearing this, one of them adds, "but much harder." Sue feels the family lost touch a bit in the busy times, but began to compensate for that by making other kinds of time available in the off season.

In several ways the McCarthys and Conways resemble craftspeople. They plunge into their work, bending and twisting it, crafting it to extract as much joy and fulfillment as they can. They design the work, exercising control in ways that change according to their own changing predilections. As in crafts the lines between work and the rest of life are blurry—it's hard to see where one begins and the other ends.

Also like the craftspeople, the innkeepers have to incorporate teaching as a part of their work. Like the buyers of crafts, guests at an inn may need to learn about it before they appreciate it. One reason why the Tamworth limits advertising is that a more general distribution of ads would reach increased numbers of the metropolitan mammal called "motelers."

Bill claims, "I can usually spot 'em when they walk in the door. They look around, kind of funny, poking around in the living rooms. There are lots of people who have no idea what an inn is, and I usually show them a room just to be sure we have no large misunderstandings. They usually like things once they understand, but there are some people who just prefer a motel and that's that." Bill says this incredulously, as if he were saying "There are some people who prefer to hang from their toes."

"The clincher for lots of them comes when we tell them they have a room with a bath down the hall. We have some people who just can't believe that, they never heard of it. And then we have a number who understand it but strongly disapprove. Like when they leave, I sometimes check to make sure the bathroom has a door on it."

Those who stay may, like any converts, become the most enthusiastic proponents of the form, taking a prominent position, shoeless, in one of the living rooms, reading in the warmth of a fireplace. They also carry the torch of the most effective kind of advertising, bringing friends back with them on inevitable later visits.

Based on the activities of such converts, and on the similar work of the more hard-core inn-stayers, the Tamworth has developed itself to a level of comfortably high activity in the inn and the restaurant. For its owners it's been pretty much a feel-your-way process and likely will continue in much the same way. The McCarthys joined some innkeeping associations but didn't keep up in them because there didn't seem to be much that they could do. The situation of the Tamworth differed too much from that of any of the others, and the McCarthys finally decided that "the best thing we could do was to promote our own inn and mind our business."

As a business the inn is close to people's whole lives —to their families, their friends, their selves—and thus offers a unique kind of opportunity for a personal integration on all fronts. The McCarthys and the Conways exemplify one path for carrying this out, but it should be clear that such integration can take place even in a business like retailing where the work does not necessarily reach into one's life. Two examples of retailing and its possible execution are explored in the following profile.

BREAD ROSES AND THE THIRD DAY

Records and plants would seem to be appealing choices for products around which to build a collectively run retail business. They lack the mystique and potential for personal involvement offered by crafts that people can actually make, but they are both products that sellers in this era can invest a measure of interest and pride.

The members of Washington's record collective Bread and Roses sometimes worry if selling records and being involved with music is politically worthy, and they extend the day-to-day business of selling records as much as they can to politicize it according to their interests. They worked with a nearby radio station, doing a weekly show, providing support for the news staff, and influencing the choice of public service ads until the institution that sponsored the station did some critical listening and pulled the plug. Recently Bread and Roses has also become involved with sponsoring live performances of musicians whose work has a political slant.

The Third Day Plant Store, located a few blocks from Bread and Roses, has a similar penchant for reaching out beyond the normal realm of selling plants. They have contributed to a recycling center, a neighborhood park, and an urban ecology education program. At bottom, though, both businesses express their politics and their personalities a bit in the product. A woman at Third Day (which takes its name from the Biblical reference, "and on the Third Day He created . . .") remarks, "The affirmation of life that is plants is my chief concern." Workers at Bread and Roses believe that some kinds of music are extremely important politically, and even music that isn't can be worthwhile.

By paying specific attention to their relationships with various pieces of the outside world, both shops also try to express their members' personalities and politics in the way they conduct the business of retailing. Bread and Roses' dealings with wholesalers, for example, have traditionally tended toward the unorthodox. Initially wholesalers didn't know what to make of the collective, as sales reps who came in to visit were put off or perhaps simply confused by what they saw in the shop. It was difficult for them to get a credit line with the suppliers, and that difficulty was exacerbated by the track record of other collectives in the area.

Bread and Roses was handling the major labels on a cash basis, which was very difficult because it tied up too much of their limited capital in stock. They finally got credit unexpectedly when they sent some records back to the companies COD and the companies, apparently unable to deal with such a maneuver, responded by opening a credit line for them. This in turn triggered the opening of credit lines from other companies. Ed Evans, a member of Bread and Roses, explains the rationale of credit: "To get any friends at all, you have to owe a lot of people money."

Now, even despite the credit lines, Bread and Roses' relationship with suppliers is not idyllic. Their refusal to promote in the store what the record companies push has not earned them any points for popularity and, besides, they usually find it most convenient to get their records from a one-stop wholesaler in Philadelphia. He handles a variety of labels, and the clientele of Bread and Roses is generally not much interested in the recent major hits. "We might only sell one or two copies of a million seller pop album," Evans observes. "Our customers' tastes usually are more selective."

The Third Day's relations with wholesalers are distinguished from their colleagues' in the plant business more by their cordiality than their awkwardness. Third Day got its start before plants became a universal element of home decorating, so most suppliers treat them with the respect due someone who's been on board since the good old days. The collective nurtures that kind of relationship by paying extra attention to the job assignment of ordering. On the opposite end, the growers have taken an interest in the shop following an initial intrigue spurred by the rotation of jobs. A member explains, "I'd call up and say, 'This is Phil,' and the grower would ask, 'So what happened to Janet?' They were fascinated by the way we bounced things around and we talked with them quite a bit."

Bread and Roses and The Third Day also devote extra attention to their relationships at the other end of the business, with customers. Like a group of craftspeople, The Third Day incorporates an element of education into the sales transaction, providing detailed information on the care, feeding, and lore of the plants it sells. The education may include a lesson in human interaction if customers are bossy. "Do this, do that, shine my shoes," a member of the group mimics an obnoxious customer. "And then when you don't jump it's 'Hey girl, where's the manager?' We try to explain things reasonably, but for some people you have to just put your foot down. I can't imagine how it would be to sell anything if the customer were always right."

Customers at Bread and Roses don't usually get an education about music (in fact, one worker believes that the store's customers are "very serious" about how they take their music) but they are treated differently than in other stores. The shop keeps used records on hand for 50¢ so that the hard-core music people can always afford to buy something. Unlike other stores, which deal with shoplifting by the rule "an eye for an eye," Bread and Roses is more gentle. Evans remarks, "Theft gets to be a problem sometimes, but we still would never press charges. What anyone could do to harm us is like nothing we could do to harm them."

As in most collectives the internal concerns are the

most difficult to resolve. Both shops have encountered the standard range of group problems: sharing knowledge, burning out, confronting each other without taking offense, making problems discussable, discouraging self-elected martyrdom. The Third Day worked with a facilitator (a person who helped them improve interpersonal communication) for a period of time and generally found the experience helpful, but its group problems have been a little more extreme than the norm; a love triangle episode being especially difficult.

Third Day shifted recently to hold a predominant concern for business. That has upset one long-time member and spurred his resignation, though it seems to be fulfilling the interests of the others. Phil Herbert left the collective amicably—he still helps out by doing their accounting—because he felt the business emphasis was "too shallow" and also because some members who were particularly important to him had left. In addition, he felt himself "losing the energy within this group to deal with fellow collective members in a creative way."

He can understand the feeling of many other members that some of the concerns of the collective process became ends in themselves, aptly described by the label "self-indulgent." Yet he also feels that they were too quick to apply the label and that, for example, the fifteen minutes they allocated for self-criticism at the end of their meetings was inadequate. At the very least, he believes it is important to be more sensitive to group process as a way of preventing calamities. He speculates that unless people take the group into some account and keep lines of communication open "pretty soon they're either not speaking to each other. The problems get so complex that they become impossible to understand."

Bread and Roses's group problems run more to the structural issues, at least at this time in its evolution. Its big issue currently is scheduling the store openings to meet the time demands of group members, two of whom work full-time and four of whom work part-time. The Third Day's eight members are all part-time, working between 25 and 35 hours per week. The shop also is searching for a way to have the part-timers carry more of the continuity of the work.

Both shops embody organizational features much like those in other collectives: members choose which tasks they want to do and usually rotate jobs, salaries are minimal but livable ($3.60 per hour at the Third Day, about $100 for a full-time thirty-two-hour week at Bread and Roses); frequent, regular meetings are the official forum for setting policies and keeping the business running smoothly. Both shops try to be sensitive to the interests of the community in which they are located, but both place their work first, designating themselves work collectives rather than community stores.

Unlike some other collectives, both shops have reached a level of financial stability. Bread and Roses did about $100,000 in sales in fiscal 1975 and projects doing about $135,000 in 1976. Like The Third Day, it is paying off the loans it took out to get off the ground. Neither shop is exactly trouble-free—in fact the crises often fly hot and heavy at both—but both are beyond the reach of beginners' awkwardness ("The best way to learn," claims Ed Evans, "is to make mistakes") and at a plateau of stability where every problem isn't a threat to survival.

Both shops owe a measure of their success to support from other, different groups. Strongforce, a group that provides various support services for work col-

lectives, helped provide $1,800 of Bread and Roses'
initial capital of $2,300 and has continued to help by
giving advice on technical matters like accounting and
law and in equally important, less specific areas like
group process. Strongforce is a part of the D.C. area
network of work collectives that has augmented the
network significantly by soliciting loan funds from
sympathetic individuals and groups, not the least of
which has been the Metro Center of the National Institute of Mental Health, a federal agency interested in
fostering the growth of alternative work organizations
in cities.

The Third Day got its support from a very different
source. The Community of Christ, a church group that
had a "dream fund," provided loans for several thousand
dollars for what a member of the group unabashedly
referred to as "seed money." The church actually re-
tains formal ownership of Third Day, but members of
the shop say they leave management pretty much up
to the shop group. The church provided the nucleus
of a support group, including community people and
Third Day staff who lend some of the moral support
Strongforce provides for other collectives. The support group meets regularly, and with increasing frequency in difficult times.

Both shops need support not only because of the
vagaries of running a collective business, but also
because the products they sell are subject to many
difficulties. Plants have a way of withering matched
only by vinyl's propensity for shortages. To combat
bate the vinyl shortage problem, Bread and Roses
approaches business at a breakneck pace, turning over
the stock two or three times a month in the limited con-
fines of their basement quarters.

Despite the problems of both businesses, members

of each group contend that their stock in trade is appropriate for collective business because of the ease of
start-up, and the possibility of getting off the ground
with relatively limited capital. Both groups have
managed to augment their low-profile approach to
business by turning up bargain rentals in a location
not well known for reasonable real estate, and Bread
and Roses has drawn significantly from the efforts of
volunteers who put in time at the store simply because
"they like it."

Bread and Roses and the Third Day have adhered
to the notion of themselves as the loci of their groups
rather than trying to become community stores or
building informal response mechanisms to the inputs
of volunteers. Much satisfaction can be derived from
this kind of independence, but there is also a special
kind of satisfaction in further blurring customer-worker
relations. The collective staff of the Boston Food
Co-op, for example, are essentially members of the co-
op who also work. In some ways they are constrained
by the membership (and especially the board of directors) but in other ways they are liberated.

THE COLLECTIVE STAFF OF THE BOSTON FOOD CO-OP

As if she were describing a traditional career in a profession or business, Anne Strong (not her real name)
recalls, "I always knew I would work in a food co-op
someday." Ms. Strong is a recent addition to the collective staff of the Boston Food Co-op, the largest food
co-op in eastern New England. She is one of a half
dozen staffers who are organized as a collective but
who, unlike those in many organizations described in
this book, are employees who are supervised to some

extent by others. The co-op is a voluntary organization run by its membership through an elected board of directors.

The collective controls the operations of the store within the constraints of policy decisions made by the board, and the operations of the store include considerable breadth and flexibility. Ms. Strong is able to draw extensively from the knowledge of food she acquired in California running a fruit stand for several years and starting an "old timey bakery" in a restored historic village. When she moved east recently, she took a clerical job but became active in the co-op community. She joined the Cambridge Co-op, and began working at the Boston Food Co-op several months later. "I didn't want to work for a government or business," she remarks. "Co-ops seemed to be a way to earn a living and still do things politically, and with people."

Doing things politically, and with people, is an appealing notion, but it tends to get a bit watered down and complicated when traced to specifics. The co-op implies some contact with people, as the staff must relate to the membership. This occurs in a direct way at the Boston Food Co-op when members put in their mandatory two hours of work per month in the store—they usually approach whatever staff is on hand and ask where they can work. Members also encounter staff on various committees, informally on the co-op floor and socially at softball games, open houses, and boogies. For many members, contact with the staff is contact with the co-op. The staff is always on hand at the co-op, they answer questions, they are in touch with the organization.

Anne Strong sees no problem in her relationships with members: "We depend on members for help, and they come to help and shop. There aren't any major conflicts." Most other members of the collective agree, but Ken Allen, a member who has been sitting in on staff meetings as a consultant, thought that staff didn't reach out to members. "They were friendly faces, the collective, but they were like statues. They didn't take the initiative," he thinks. He speculates that some staffers may not reach out because they are afraid their reaching may be seen as grabbing. They don't want to isolate or irritate members, and may be so concerned with not coming on strong that they don't come on at all.

If the co-op were not a membership organization, it would be acceptable for staffers to not reach out, but the needs of the co-op are clearly oriented toward broader involvement. Besides, the membership aspect of the co-op is a plus for many members of the collective who, like Anne Strong, thrive on the human contact the membership provides. "Organizing the membership is part of this job," she notes. The task for members of the collective is not an easy one, though, as it entails both accumulating the knowledge necessary to run the co-op and accurately imparting that knowledge to the membership so they can share in it and, if they choose, reshape it.

Staffers sometimes feel that the considered judgments of their experience are tossed out the window so that the board can experiment, possibly jeopardizing the co-op. Most frequently, conflicts do not occur directly between the staff and the membership but between the staff and the board of directors elected by the membership. The relationship between the board and the staff has had a stormy history dating back even to the first board and the first staffer.

The conflict between the board and the staff is understandable and perhaps inevitable. The collective is in a position of intense involvement with the operation

of the co-op; that is their job, their raison d'être. It is
what they know best and care about most. Because
of their involvement, they often know more than the
board. Staffers sometimes complain that board members simply don't know the co-op, and that they add
insult to this ignorance by disdaining to learn. Typically, staffers contend that board members don't like to
"get their hands dirty" and that they are overly interested in theory and abstraction. Further, some staffers
argue, the board used to at least draw from people with
much hands-on experience in the co-op, but the co-op's
increasing growth and popularity has made board membership somewhat of a "status" activity and thus
attracted some people not concerned chiefly with the
co-op.

Meanwhile, board members argue that staffers can't
see the larger meanings of the co-op because they are
too engrossed in getting through a work day. Both
staffers and board anchor their arguments in their
legitimacy as representatives of membership—staffers
by dint of direct contact with members, and board members via the formal election process.

Most unfortunately, both sides at times seem determined to make the worst of what the logistics of the
arrangement imply will necessarily be a tricky situation.
Matters recently took a downturn during the employee
review process, an activity the board and the members
conduct as a way of evaluating staffers.

The concept of peer review itself did not disturb
staffers who seemed to recognize the legitimacy of
some kind of review. However, staffers were infuriated
with the quantitative bent of the review process, which
they claimed was typical of the academically minded
board. "They're trying to tape measure us," a staffer
complains. "You can't tape measure people." In addi-

tion, some board members felt the whole process was a sham, an attempt to objectify the wish of some people on the board to get rid of some people in the staff. A big flap developed over the second review, and none has been held since.

Some members of the collective view the board's review effort as much as an indicator of their own lack of organization and initiative as of their problems with the board. They see the collective's acceptance of the review process as the real problem, believing that the staff should have (and could have) had more input into the process. One staffer observes, "The idea of worker control is not here at all." There is some argument to be made that the staff has paid attention to its own organization only as much as the operating of the store has forced it to.

Looking more closely, it soon becomes apparent that problems of communication within the staff mirror many of the difficulties the staff has with the board. "We're not as honest with others as we could be," one staffer thinks. "We're good at talking about each other, but not to the people we're talking about. That does seem to be changing, but it's happening slowly. We should be able to bullshit about each other to each other in an honest way."

The collective's acceptance (though reluctant at first) of Ken Allen is also some evidence of their growing concern for their organization. Some believe he is at least partially responsible for the positive change in the group. He is known around the co-op as the "in-house metaphysician," a title he seems to enjoy. The simple physical presence of someone whose concern is the group's functioning works the concern into everyone's mind. At times the situation is a bit awkward, like a priest at a party, but the consultant is sure of himself and the group has accepted him. He has not yet intruded in meetings that he attends or interactions that he observes, but has made himself available and found that people do come and talk with him. He is concerned with how citizens, members of the co-op, can learn to act as resources for one another.

Allen has done a lot of watching, and has quite a bit of insight into the group's problems. One issue that seemed particularly important to him was the group's meetings, which are held weekly and often run upward of four hours. The meetings carry the torch of tradition handed down from left politics that seems to mandate cross-talking, little listening, and exasperation. "Meetings were catatonic. People hardly paid attention to what the meetings were about," Allen recalls. "There was a phone nearby, and it rang a lot. People used it as one of many excuses to get up and walk around. They'd come and go during a meeting; there was no continuity. When they finally did get around to talking, they often would trash each other. It's not that they were trying to hurt each other, or that it was intentional, but that meetings had a history of scarring people, and being generally unpleasant and unproductive."

Despite their best intentions, it is difficult for members of the group to change their feelings about and their behavior in meetings and their more general sense of collectivism. Some staffers believe that "the purpose of meetings is to give people headaches. You sign up, sit in a room, and get a headache." They think the real work of the co-op gets done in informal ad hoc meetings during the day. Still, they are generally convinced of the importance of what Ken Allen is trying to bring about.

Members of the collective are very vocal about their preferences for working in the unique social milieu of the co-op and very aware of the political nature of their work. One notes, "We've got to have a real alternative here. It can't be the same as regular life, except that we wear overalls." Many of them strongly support the necessity for a board of directors to feasibly represent the membership. Yet they don't seem to have gotten beyond working within the co-op as a group of individuals connected only loosely to each other and to the larger group.

In this context, communication is not a luxury but an absolutely necessary foundation for job satisfaction. Work in the co-op demands a high level of involvement. One doesn't function as a member of the collective with an attachment to bankers' hours—it is fully expected that staffers attend meetings, social events, and regional co-op activities, and staffers usually do all this because they want to. But when such high involvement is the norm, it should not be expected to come without a price.

The price the co-op pays for the high involvement of staffers is the staffers' high demand for input. The nature of the work implies that they must engage in a serious search for the best possible ways of getting things done, their high involvement leading them to feel they have a right to such input. The involvement itself is not the issue—staffers wouldn't have it any other way. The issue is that for members of the collective, control over their work stretches far and wide. Wherever they stretch, staffers' interests seem most likely to reflect concerns directly related to the operations of the store. It is when this concern is perceived to conflict with others that the nature of the co-op is called into question.

A sociologist who did her doctoral dissertation on a large New England co-op noted that "nearly every major decision about how to solve these (organizational) problems was determined by criteria of economic efficiency in spite of their being couched in terms of ideological debate."[5] People with influence in the co-op have almost always placed co-op operations first, thus assuming a fairly conservative business profile, especially when compared with other alternative economic organizations. Current members of the Boston Food Co-op collective give the opposite opinion, contending that they are always taking organizational risks that astonish accountant friends.

Control is at issue here, and it is important to identify this control in terms of the politics of co-op operations and in terms of the classic concept of workers' control that a substantial research literature persuasively links with job satisfaction. Workers' control of their work environment, the argument goes, is essential for job satisfaction. The BFC collective allows for a considerable amount of control by its members, who pick their own schedules and tasks and have much latitude in executing the work they do.

The question thus arises, how much control is necessary for job satisfaction, and the answer in the co-op is quite complex. For a job which has few links to a worker's deep personal involvement, a few basic kinds of control may well be adequate—not everyone wants complete immersion in his or her work. However, some people do want to be immersed in their work, and that is the initial profile the co-op presents as a work environment. Members of the collective are not expected by their colleagues, the membership, on the board to be "nine-to-fivers" but at times to eat, drink, and live co-op. Work on the collective is carried out as an act of love and art, and in such a context the prospects for any kind of supervision are not very good. The policy issues on which the co-op board rules might be expected, therefore, to have a much greater significance for members of the collective than the decisions of A & P's board has for its employees.

Within the current arrangement, staffers exert considerable control over a swath of concerns related to store operations. Each staffer is supposed to be responsible for one product area (such as produce, cheese, groceries), taking on the work of all aspects of the product in the store: inventory, ordering, sales, display, bookkeeping. This arrangement has had important implications for staffers' work, enabling them to become experts in an area. The arrangement has also simplified management somewhat, defining accountability and responsibility more clearly than the previous arrangements.

The current organization of work in the co-op creates "whole" jobs for members of the collective, reinforcing in the structure of the work the tradition and group norms for involvement. All this helps develop efficiency and technical expertise, but it loads interactions between staff and both the membership and the board. "Whole" jobs concentrate the knowledge of operating the co-op in the hands and minds of staffers so that members' work usually entails little or no risk. The broader the scope of staffers' work as defined by its structure and level of commitment, the narrower is the work left to be done by members. BFC has attempted to limit this sort of thing by consciously and successfully, striving to have members assume positions of responsibility. Several departments are run almost entirely by members. Whole jobs affect the collective's relationship with the board by underscoring a staffer's need to define jobs broadly, potentially encroaching on the concerns of the board.

Other issues of work aside from the structure of whole

jobs and the dilemmas of communication contribute to
making work at the co-op potentially very enjoyable.
The tone of things in general at the co-op is generally
very friendly. Staffers respond without questioning
to each other's short-term emergencies, accomplishing
schedule changes and alterations in work structure in
a matter of minutes when it is necessary. Staffers are
paid between $100 and $150 per week, depending on
need. The group defines need itself in response to the
proposals and requests of staffers. Staffers get one
week of paid vacation for each six months of work they
put in. At present, people have their own health insurance from outside, but that may be altered if people's
needs change.

Staffers determine their own schedules, putting in
four blocks of seven hours each of formal work in addition to whatever time they spend informally at the co-op.
Schedules are reviewed and work assignments checked
out at the weekly meetings, the transient source of most
current co-op knowledge. The schedule gets the work
of the co-op done within a framework of always trying
to have at least two staffers in the store at all times.
The schedule's flexibility helps accommodate people
who need or want to change their schedules frequently
and people with "chronically" difficult time demands,
like the working parent of two who is the co-op's "produce person." She fits her hours around the school
schedules of her children.

Unfortunately, the long-term prospects for staffers
seem as dim as the short-term aspects seem bright.
Development and change are accomplished only with
difficulty, so much so that it is often necessary to leave
in order to change. The nature of the group currently
reinforces this kind of stability, engaging in a process
of labeling that is powerful and inflexible. Once

staffers acquire a reputation for one or another trait, others are slow to see them in any other way. This sort of labeling is rooted in individual and group needs for some sort of stability in the face of massive change and transiency, but the reasons do not solve the problem. Perhaps the numbers of people and the level of activity at the co-op place this problem beyond solution.

Rather than changing in the co-op, the normal path for growth and development seems to lead to a period of catatonia after co-op work. Staffers characteristically "burn out" as a culmination of their co-op experience, leaving to cool their heels in a rural cabin for a few years. There is certainly an absence of clear development alternatives, no visible set of career tracks that offer much in the way of clearness or appeal. Some early staffers who burned out reappeared in other co-ops, but some others made dramatic shifts. One keystone of the Boston co-op community is now an investment banker in New York; another owns and operates a bustling apartment rental business in Boston. The co-op places people in the difficult developmental position of not allowing them to change while they are in it and not helping them to grow through it. People who leave benefit from the change and are often able to make important discoveries about themselves, but the co-op loses out in its failure to engage their knowledge and experience. The "membership" category provides a handy bullpen for workers in the wings, but it is much removed from the "real" stuff.

There is also some reason for believing that the pattern of staff transiency will change as a result of the co-op's move away from its warehouse on the Boston University campus to a former tire store in Allston, a blue-collar urban neighborhood—leaving the university community altered the make-up of the membership, because students have generally found the new location inconvenient and neighborhood people have replaced the students. As these changes begin to be reflected in the staff, the group's median age will likely go up. Most staffers are now thirty or under; if the median age increases, the group's patterns of needs and development will likely change also.

The move to Allston has generally been beneficial for the co-op, offering it an opportunity for renewal and revitalization, a chance to shake off ties with the university community and to try out the co-op in a different environment. It took a good deal of material and psychic energy to get through the move—the new building had to be cleaned and painted, which kept lots of people busy for months. Now sales are leveling off and the store seems to be acquiring some stability. There was some conflict at the initiation of the move, attributing it to politics within the university. Now, however, the consensus is that whatever pushed the co-op was fortunate. A staffer explains: "Because the nature of the co-op is to procrastinate, it may have been the best thing to happen to us."

There are those who think that the current organization of the co-op is top-heavy, that a business the size of the co-op (and especially one with a claim to help from volunteers) can get along on fewer staff. There are also those who believe that the staff has become less people-oriented as burned-out "people-people" are replaced by "business-people." These dilemmas, along with the chronic puzzle of relationships with the membership, will no doubt continue to plague the co-op in years to come, but the key word in this notion seems not to be "dilemma" but "continue."

THAT'S ENTERTAINMENT: MAINE STREET/
THE POOBLEY-GREEGY PUPPET THEATER

The lines distinguishing work from the rest of life seem
to reach their blurriest for the work of the theater. In
one sense this blurring is a pleasant myopia like that of
the several members of Maine Street, a mime group.
"We know each other too well now," one of them observes. "It's hard to put on a work face. You begin
a routine and you can't get through it because you look
at each other and break into giggles." Just what it is
that comprises a "work face" is not entirely clear, but
for some reason it is riotously funny (and seemingly
normal) when a member of the group answers the door
during the interview and lays a routine on the good-
natured U.P.S. person.

Steve and Jan Babcock, the founders of the Poobley-
Greegy Puppet Theater, also occasionally lapse into
routines in response to an inadvertent reference to a
part of their show. Like the magic word on the Groucho
Marx show, the right sounds can divert a conversation.
After a while, it grows difficult to separate the real and
theatrical parts of the conversation.

It's a classic theatrical dilemma of "living the part,"
and it has a few light moments, but it also has some
difficult ones. Mixing oneself up in one's work to the
extent demanded in the theater also produces an extreme
kind of vulnerability. "If I fail," Jan Babcock remarks,
"I fail the show, I fail Steve, and I fail myself. It's
very scary." Living the part, then, doesn't mean only
having a few moments of fantasy occasionally mixing
with reality; it also means taking it on the chin when the
part has any difficulties. Of course, it is theoretically
possible for people to not live a part, but very difficult
to divest themselves of deep involvement with their

work because they have often put much time and preparation into it. Steve Babcock has dabbled in puppetry
since his childhood; he and Janice spent months preparing a show, creating the puppets and the stage in
addition to writing the script. Similarly, Maine Street
members spent months in mime school and more months
rehearsing in a hall that they were able to use free of
charge in Norway, Maine.

Bad reviews and failure on the set comprise one kind
of difficulty with the role, a kind that focuses largely
on self and ego. These are serious, but a near luxury
sort of affliction, like gout, that are felt only by a select
few, those who have managed to get a part to play.
For both Maine Street and Poobley-Greegy, getting
a part has meant creating one; both have developed
their own acts rather than enlisting in traditional productions. A member of Maine Street explains, "If we
had gone the 'legit theater' route, we would be far lower
on the scale and have gotten much less experience."
Stock productions apparently are few and far between,
and the supply of actors usually far exceeds the demand.
Further, a woman member of the group pointed out that
the plight of women is especially difficult: "There are
many more women in the theater than men, but there
are usually more parts for men."

Maine Street is able to provide a broader range of
experience for its members than the bit parts they might
be lucky to find elsewhere. They have a repertoire
of routines they've presented at dinner theaters, crafts
shows, restaurants, and as warm-ups for "legit" productions. They had some bookings on a college circuit,
and were also thinking about experimenting with street
theater. Early in their brief history they worked as
singing waiters and waitresses in a resort restaurant,
squeezing their act out between dishes. They left that

after a short time because "the quality of the show was suffering, and we were getting too proud to deal with compromising our act."

One of Maine Street's biggest problems has been simply finding work. Its members are not easily categorized among traditional ranks of entertainers, and even if they were, those ranks are not easily broken into. A member relates one of the vagaries of getting work: "There was this one place that we kept calling and calling to get an audition. They always rejected us. But then, somebody who saw us told the manager there that we were good. He called us, and we were hired."

The problems of "breaking in" are often compounded by the uncertainties of show business itself. Maine Street, for example, moved to Cape Cod with a signed contract for work. "We did everything right and everything went wrong," one member remarks. They rented a house and got all settled, only to have their employer default on the contract. They spent the rest of the summer making ends meet with short gigs at other places, and managed to pull through without starving and with a significant amount of experience.

Steve and Jan Babcock have had similar problems getting work until they were hired, indirectly, by the government. The Poobley-Greegy Puppet Theater has had its traveling show (to grammar schools around the state) financed by the Massachusetts Bicentennial Commission and a grant from the federal government, with matching money put up by local school boards. "It was a real scramble getting funds, beginning with securing the Commission's approval and continuing with reverberations from every fiscal crisis the state has weathered. It's extremely difficult for a state under financial pressures to justify any spending on puppets."

The Babcocks have managed to make a living by their work, though, and it is with considerable pride that they point out that, "This is the first time that we're earning a living from doing the work we want to do."

COMMON STOCK RESTAURANT

Food aside, one of the most striking features of Common Stock is the way it looks. It's located in what used to be a hobby shop in an old building in the center of Waltham, Massachusetts. There's a bright yellow awning, a piano just inside the door (which gets frequent use from customers), a natural brick wall that harbors a small exhibit of the works of local artists, natural wood floors, and solid old tables and chairs. The chalkboard menu lists a variety of natural vegetarian foods, some of which sound extremely tasty. There's a crowd of people at lunchtime, a mix of office workers, students, and just about everything else.

During the group's daily meeting the problems and high points of the day were discussed and rehashed. Several members of the group got a round of applause for their outstanding efforts, one got the raspberries for a problem. Two members who jointly designed an odd triangular table to experiment with more efficient seating arrangements got both applause and raspberries; the former as appreciation for the effort, the latter because the table was strange.

Before my interview with the group started, they indulged in a little fantasizing on the subject of tabouli. Several members of the group had realized that tabouli was popular beyond all proportion of what they took people's knowledge of it to be. Their theory was that people ordered tabouli because it had an interesting name, and didn't know what it really was. Someone suggested seizing on tabouli's intrigue and mass-marketing it. There could be tabouli burgers, big taboulis, tabouli and fries, tabouli and a thick shake, a whole chain of fast tabouli restaurants.

WR When did you move into the building? It's really in beautiful shape.

CS We found it in the summer of 1974, and that's when we started renting. We did renovation work for nine months. It was a shoe store since 1910, then more recently it was a hobby shop. Five or seven of us worked on the store every day, and the other half dozen had regular jobs that helped support the workforce.

WR How did you get started, and when? I presume you had some kind of background of working together before taking on anything like this.

CS The thirteen people originally got together as part of a larger group, a political action project that was part of the Honeywell campaign. It was called DDT, the Daily Death Toll. About 35 or 40 people in 1971, 1972, and even earlier were organizing against the war. We focused on Honeywell because they made antipersonnel weapons.

WR You had a shared interest in politics, then. How did you get from there to here?

CS Six people in that group wanted to do a restaurant and got one started, the Hedge School, at Boston University. They passed that restaurant on to another group but its success kept the idea alive in the larger group and made an example for us.

WR How much capital did it take you to get started? One thing that has amazed me in writing this book is the extremely high cost of getting any kind of business off the ground. You spent a couple of months of your time working here to get the build-ing in shape. How much do you figure it cost to open?

CS Between $20,000 and $25,000, but that included paying a few of us a subsistence salary while we renovated. The only people we had to hire out-side the collective were a licensed plumber and electrician and that was expensive. The total included supplies and materials to open too.

WR Where did the money come from? Did you get bank loans, or was it your own savings? That sounds like a lot of money.

CS We got small no-interest loans from friends, a grant from a Quaker sharing group in upstate New York, and we got a loan from the Haymarket Foundation. We also got some money by fund-raising by having benefits and mailings. We thought we had enough at one point, but at the end we had to borrow some money from friends. Overall, we got most of our money from friends.

WR It's been a few years now since you got started. Where do you stand now? How many people are active and full-time?

CS The original collective was thirteen, but three of that group have left for various reasons. A number of people work here who are not collec-tive members. About five people work full-time.

WR How much do people get paid?

CS Fifteen dollars a day, and a day is about a seven-hour shift. We do dinners on weekends now, so there is a late shift on those days. Some people "float" with their days, but about five of us have a regular part-time schedule. One of the part-timers works her daily schedule here around her kids' school schedule. The fifteen dollars isn't always enough, so some of us take on work outside occasionally.

WR What does the financial picture look like for restaurants? Other groups that I've seen are in businesses where it seems pretty easy to keep track of costs. It would seem that there is more "slippage" in dealing with food; it might be hard to keep track of, between ordering, preparing and getting it on the plate.

CS It is difficult. We try and get around it by making some of the jobs, like bookkeeping and ordering food, rotate less frequently than the others so people can get used to them and there can be less upset. One thing we want to change with our finances is our hours. We want to be open more, so we can bring in a little more money. We do a good business for the time that we're open, but we're open for limited hours compared to other restaurants. Initially that was O.K. for what people wanted, but I think we want a little more work time now.

WR What else can you do to alter your finances? Is there anything else?

CS We can raise our prices, but we don't want to do that. We like to make the kind of food we sell accessible.

WR You seem to project a love for the food. I think I'm getting hungry. Do you have any specialties that you're especially fond of?

CS We do a very good carrot cake, a lot of stuffed vegetables, an excellent three-cheese quiche.

WR How do you make sure it tastes good, if you rotate jobs? I know you have recipes, but I also know there's a lot of space between the recipe and what you eat.

CS We meet every day and go over the feedback we got—we always talk to customers, so we have some feel for things. Today, for example, we found a few people who thought the pieces of quiche were too small.

WR It's great to have that kind of relationship with customers. How do you do at the other end, with suppliers? They can be pretty hard-nosed.

CS Some of them laugh at the kind of food we have when they come in, but most of them are helpful and friendly. They sit down and have a cup of coffee, and they seem to enjoy the sight of so many people running around to run a restaurant. My favorite was this one delivery person who always made us his last stop so he could spend a little time playing the piano. He was really quite good; we all enjoyed it.

Like all the groups in this chapter and the chapter on professions, Common Stock has crafted and designed its relationships. Common Stock is noteworthy among the groups for the burden of its high level of capitalization, but it is possible to see the capitalization in a positive way because of the strength it lends to the group in the long run. It is an obligation, but one to which members of the group willingly submit.

The groups in this chapter depict a range of varying levels of commitment, size, capitalization, production processes, relationships with the outside world and among themselves, concern for personal expression, and ingenuity. All have tailored the work they do to their own needs, and usually in a way that personalizes it. At IGP, personalizing the work largely means making it less oppressive by altering its timing and surroundings. In some of the other groups, personalizing the work means ripping it apart and rebuilding it in a way that other traditional "practitioners" might not recognize.

By depicting part of the range of possibilities for designing one's own work this book attempts not to be exhaustive but to hint at what is possible. The book could easily go on for another sixty pages, expanding on the various parameters of possibilities by describing more groups. In fact, every group I visited had made some sort of innovation in its approach to work. The end of this book, then, is really but a beginning in understanding what these groups do in designing work.

CHAPTER FIVE

Concluding Comments . . . On Organizational Learning

"The nature of the co-op is to procrastinate," a member of one group told me. She was referring to her own group's legendary penchant for agonized decision-making, but she might have also been describing many of the organizations discussed in this book. Though this description may be accurate, it is important not to view procrastination as evidence of ineffectiveness, but rather as a strategy groups may use intentionally to bring the opinions of their members to the fore.

Participatory work groups cannot be fully understood in terms of traditional measures like productivity, though their critics (and sometimes, unfortunately, their members) often use such measures as evidence of a group's ineffectiveness. Productivity, efficiency, and profit are not necessarily relevant goals for participatory work groups, but are among the variables from which members may (or may not) choose when they do set goals, variables subject to the group's exercise of control. The groups define effectiveness in their own terms, and those will include their own approaches to efficiency and productivity.

The preceding chapters ought to have made clear the special vitality and ingenuity of participatory work groups. Here I want to stress that vitality as a foundation for a general understanding of the groups, and to suggest that that general understanding take as central the notion of "organizational learning"[1] rather than other traditional measures of performance. Learning is more complex, more varied, and hence more suited to mirror the complexity of the groups themselves.

Learning can assume many forms for organizations, as it can for individuals. A furniture company can learn to produce tables more rapidly, an automobile company can learn to produce cars more inexpensively. A participatory work group may similarly learn to increase its productive capacity in one way or another, but it may also learn *about* productive capacity, to question whether production is what it wants to be doing at all and change it if it chooses. Learning in a hierarchical workplace, as in traditional schooling, is defined at the top by managers (teachers). Learning in a collective is defined by the learners (members) themselves.

All the members of a participatory work group can scrutinize their learning in a way that only the managers of a hierarchical workplace can. Collectives not only solve problems, they also *set* them. There are some baseline levels necessary for group survival but beyond that, the group can define its own purposes. The groups detailed in Chapter 3, for example, all set the problems of their respective professions in ways that differed significantly from the mainstream.

The participatory structure places members in a different position with respect to learning than they would have in a hierarchy: every member of a collective is an executive, everyone is justifiably concerned with every aspect of the group. Members may organize to break down some of this sharing, but they can also organize to restore it or to maximize it.

As long as the groups can set their own objectives, it is important for them to learn to do so to mirror the interests of their members. Often the most critical factor in these choices is recognizing that they exist in the first place. It is a testimony to the power of traditional values that groups avowedly most concerned for the personal growth and development of their members often take on too much work to allow that cultivation to occur. Learning to schedule, then, is an important task that must take into account workloads, stress, members' convenience, and contact with the outside world.

As with individuals, the most important kind of learning for groups is learning to learn.[2] The full potential of a co-operative lies in its ability to involve all its members meaningfully and thus to surface in the group the ideas of all the individuals. Some of the groups in this book try to make it a matter of course that members criticize each other freely, informally during the normal activities of the working day, and formally at meetings. Such criticism and openness in everyday organizational life can help make it easier for people to question many aspects of the group, then, by creating an environment in which it is acceptable for individuals to raise issues of importance to them. In addition, an open environment can enable the members to go beyond individual questioning to a joint, mutual exploration that produces from the interaction ideas no one person would have developed.

Organizational learning for a participatory work group consists, overall, in raising issues, making them the subject of real discussion and deliberation, and resolving them in ways consistent with the group's interests. Groups engaged in this process are conducting research into their own practice, carefully and continually. This task is not easy, but the groups described in this text have made some impressive attempts to work it out. The charts included in the appendix represent one way of undertaking such research.

The mechanics of a group researching into its own practice often cause problems.[3] It is not research in the impersonal sense, but quite the opposite, extremely personal and very difficult to discuss. Yet it is precisely this kind of research that markedly distinguishes the participatory groups from hierarchical organizations. The challenge for co-operatives and collectives is not to perform to the standards of others, but to regard those standards as possibilities, and to strive to become aware of and place into practice their own programs for performance.

On Policy. It ought to be clear that participatory work groups offer an especially satisfying kind of work. They are flexible, loose, and thus responsive to the needs of people whom traditional jobs are apt to satisfy least, people who want more or less than the bureaucratized workplace is able to offer. The more work becomes bureaucratized and satisfying work becomes an endangered species, the more value accrues to arrangements offering alternative paths to satisfying work.

Because satisfying work is important for individuals and, in the aggregate, for society, it makes sense for social policy to foster satisfying work in whatever ways it can. A good deal of effort is already being taken to redesign jobs in large, corporate settings to achieve this end. Job redesign gives workers more autonomy and control in their work, following the premise that control is a cornerstone of job satisfaction. One could logically extend this effort to participatory work groups, co-ops, and collectives that offer in a "natural setting" what job redesign strives for (and in fact, may never ultimately attain).

Participatory work groups serve important interests for individuals and communities and are arguably legitimate components of a policy for employment. Obviously the groups are not right for everyone, but they are very right for some people. Moreover, there is some possibility that those for whom the groups are right warrant special interest. Flexible work arrangements may be able to engage those traditionally excluded from bureaucratic work—the poor, the uneducated, the unregimented. Those alienated by bureaucratic work, the social entrepreneurs and mavericks who prod society toward innovation and discovery, also may flourish in nontraditional work organizations. Research on political participation[4] shows a link between activity in small groups and more general kinds of political participation, suggesting further that participatory work groups may serve a socializing role.

Social policy supporting participatory work groups would be a "jobs" policy that stresses the content of the jobs more than current programs do, a policy that has more concern for people than the simple creation of make-work. Policy that supports ongoing arrangements also makes sense logistically, working with wheels that are already turning rather than attempting to invent them, and then striving to set them in motion.

Participatory work groups probably can't benefit much from complex support programs—they are too straightforward and too busy to get hung up in government bureaucracy. However, they could benefit greatly from simple supports, simply administered. Vouchers enabling groups to buy support services—accounting, management, and group process consulting—could go a long way toward securing direct assistance and initiating the development of services specifically attuned to participatory groups. Improved access to (and perhaps subsidy of) health insurance, capital funding, and technical assistance would all be quite helpful. Any reduction in the effort necessary for a group to maintain itself would enable it to devote more time to its central purpose, the work itself.

The Small Business Administration has falteringly carried the government's commitment to small business; seriously improving on what it already does would be most useful. In addition, there are other important ideas which might be expanded. Massachusetts' State Bank bill (currently in the works in the state legislature) would specifically earmark venture capital for co-operative activities in recognition of their special potential for community development.

Overall, the arguments for policy supporting participatory work groups are not far removed from the rationale of existing manpower policy. However, thinking about collectives and co-operatives entails thinking small, and while that is a wise, ecologically sound kind of thinking, it is not what policymakers are used to. What is called for is a policy for diversity. Small participatory work groups are diverse and unconventional. They can benefit from assistance that policy can provide, but the policy must accept and protect their diversity rather than attempting to level it off.

Notes

CHAPTER 1

1. E. F. Schumacher, *Small Is Beautiful* (New York: Harper and Row, 1973).
2. Champ Clark, "Back to the Simple Life," *Money* (August 1975).
3. *Work in America* (Cambridge, Mass.: MIT Press, 1975).
4. For example, Chapter 3 of *Work in America* cites the following references: Erdman Palmore, "Predicting Longevity: A Follow-Up Controlling for Age," *Gerontology* (1969); Sula Benet, "Why They Live To Be 100, or Even Older, in Abkhasia," *New York Times Magazine* (December 26, 1972); John R. P. French and Robert D. Caplan, "Organizational Stress and Individual Strain," in A. J. Marrow, ed., *The Failure of Success* (New York: American Management Association, 1972); M. Susser, "Causes of Peptic Ulcer: A Selective Epidemiologic Review," *Journal of Chronic Diseases* 20 (1967); S. Cobb, *The Frequency of Rheumatic Diseases* (Cambridge, Mass.: Harvard University Press, 1971); Arthur Kornhauser, *Mental Health of the Industrial Worker* (New York: Wiley, 1965).

5. Kornhauser, *Mental Health*.
6. Ibid.
7. Ibid.
8. Ibid., p. 30. The original study was published in *Occupational Mental Health* 1 (2): 1971.
9. Ibid., p. 99.
10. Cited in David Jenkins, *Job Power* (Baltimore: Penguin Books, 1974), p. 60. G. D. H. Cole, "Collectivism, Syndicalism and Guilds," in Ken Coates and Tony Topham, eds., *Workers Control* (London: Panther Modern Society, 1970), p. 47
11. Sidney Verba and Norman Nye, *Participation in America* (New York: Harper and Row, 1972), pp. 186, 191.
12. *Work in America*, p. 21.
13. County Business Patterns, 1972, Table 1C, cited in Robert N. Ray, "A Report on Self-Employed Americans in 1973," *Monthly Labor Review* (January 1975).
14. Peter Berger outlines the plight of professionals in general in *The Human Shape of Work* (New York: Macmillan, 1964) and Henri-Claude Bailly details the position of architects in part in "The Architecture Profession: An Industry?" (Harvard Business School Case 9-672-148), 1972. *Work in America* also briefly discusses professionals (pp. 21–22).
15. Ray, "Report on Self-Employed Americans."
16. Berger, *The Human Shape of Work*, p. 214.
17. *Work in America*, p. 22.
18. Tibor Scitovsky, *The Joyless Economy* (New York: Oxford University Press, 1976), p. 11. Scitovsky's insightful analysis and use of data in this book are outstanding.
19. Cited in Jenkins, *Job Power*, p. 46. The original reference was G. V. O. Osipov, ed., *Industry and Labor in the USSR* (London: Tavistock, 1966).

20. National Opinion Research Center, *General Social Survey 1973* (Williamstown, Mass.: Williams College, Roper Public Opinion Research Center, July 1973).

21. I am indebted to Lisa R. Peattie for this insight and for introducing me to the more general outlook she has developed on marginal economies and "cockroach capitalists."

22. Harry Braverman, *Labor and Monopoly Capital* (New York: Monthly Review Press, 1974).

23. Ibid., p. 114.

24. Ibid., p. 125.

25. See, for example, *Work in America*, pp. 7, 13.

26. Braverman, *Labor and Monopoly Capital*, p. 90.

27. Jane Loevinger, "Theories of Ego Development," in Louis Breger, ed., *Clinical-Cognitive Psychology* (Englewood Cliffs, N.J.: Prentice-Hall, 1969), p. 85.

28. *Work in America*, p. 1.

29. *The Philistine* can be found in numerous antique book stores, along with a number of other Hubbard publications.

30. Robert Heilbroner, *The Worldly Philosophers* (New York: Simon and Schuster, 1967), p. 32.

31. Jenkins, *Job Power*, p. 20.

CHAPTER 2

1. "Stormy Reports," *Sunshine Artists* (September 1975), pp. 19–20.

2. *Boston Globe* (July 27, 1976).

CHAPTER 3

1. Henri-Claude Bailly, "The Architecture Profession: An Industry?" (Harvard Business School Case 9-672-148), 1972.

2. Ibid., p. 2.
3. Ibid., p. 19.
4. Wilma L. Ronco, "An Alternative to the Traditional Classroom: An In-Depth Observation of One Classroom at the McCarthy-Towne School, West Acton, Massachusetts" (unpublished paper, April 1974).

CHAPTER 4

1. "Sen. Nelson Blames Government for Sad Shape of Small Business," *Boston Globe* (November 16, 1975).
2. "Is This Any Time to Start a Business?" *Changing Times* (October 1975).
3. Cited in ibid.
4. *The New Yorker* (August 16, 1975).
5. Diane S. Piktialis, "Feeding The People: A Case Study of an Alternative Economic Organization," Ph.D. dissertation, Boston University Graduate School, 1976.

CHAPTER 5

1. My understanding of organizational learning was largely developed and refined in conversations with Donald A. Schön.
2. Learning to learn is developed as an independent idea by Gregory Bateson in *Steps to an Ecology of Mind* (New York: Ballantine, 1972).
3. Chris Argyris and Donald Schön's book, *Theory in Practice* (San Francisco: Jossey-Bass, 1974), offers an extremely useful model for interaction that is particularly useful for participatory groups.
4. Sidney Verba and Norman Nye, *Participation in America* (New York: Harper and Row, 1972).

APPENDIX A

Helping Resources

For all its shortcomings, the Small Business Administration is quite good at providing information and technical assistance for people interested in creating their own jobs. There are offices of the SBA in most cities. Beyond the SBA, there are also organizations dedicated to the assistance of more specifically defined types of work. These include:

The American Crafts Council, 44 West 53rd St., New York, N.Y. 10019. The ACC has an extensive publications list, a very successful annual show, and a variety of services for craftspeople. They will send a brochure upon request. Other organizations for craftspeople operate on a more regional or local basis, and may be identified through the ACC.

Vocations for Social Change, 353 Broadway, Cambridge, Mass. 02139 publishes the *Peoples Yellow Pages* and is deeply concerned with work collectives, a subject on which they have recently compiled an informative booklet. They also offer counseling for individuals and groups, and leads to similar organizations in other parts of the country. **Strongforce**, 2121 Decatur Pl. N.W., Washington, D.C. 20008, is a D.C. incarnation of the VSC idea. It publishes *Democratic Economics*, a newsletter, and training manuals for work collectives in various types of worker-run businesses. It also counsels work collectives on technical and organizational issues. *Workforce*, published on the West Coast, serves the national perspective of collectively run concerns; it is available from 5951 Canning St., Oakland, Cal. 94609.

The Cooperative League of the US, 1828 L St. N.W., Suite 1100, Washington, D.C. 20036, is concerned with the co-op form of organizing work. It maintains extensive publications lists that could be of use to small groups.

There are a large number of books and magazines that aim to help people create their own jobs. Most seem determined to make such work as crass as possible ("Make a million dollars shampooing rugs") but two offer more insight: Claudia Jessup and Genie Chipps, *The Woman's Guide to Starting a Business* (New York: Holt, Rinehart & Winston, 1976); and the quarterly *Working Papers* (123 Mt. Auburn St., Cambridge, Mass. 02139).

APPENDIX B

Organizational
Statements

These statements are included to provide more detail
on two of the organizations described in the text, the
McCarthy-Towne School and the Open Design Studio.
The statements are products of a kind of introspective
work that seems helpful in guiding a group to an understanding and appreciation of itself. In this latter respect,
the form of Open Design's statement suggests a structure for a group's inquiry into its own practice. Both
statements represent efforts of the groups to make sense
of themselves, so the statements are interesting both in
the intricate ways in which they structure the organizations and in the group work that they symbolize.

ORGANIZATION DEVELOPMENT PROPOSAL—
McCARTHY-TOWNE SCHOOL SCHOOL

I. Statement of Intention. The Task Force on Organizational Development makes the following proposal
today with the intention of setting in motion the beginnings of a change in our internal structure.

We have worked on this proposal in the spirit of the
organizational workshop days. Attempting to meet
some of the concerns expressed during those days.

It should be understood that this proposal is based on a conceptual change in our organizational procedures. It is this basic concept which we, as a staff, must either accept or reject.

In the construction of this proposal we maintained the premise that our school's decision-making process is firmly based upon the strength of each of our faculty members (not, however, on *all* of our faculty members on all issues).

The Task Force acknowledges that our proposal is far from perfect. It encompasses both vague and specific issues and it suggests both firm and flexible ground rules. We have tried to be fair in our efforts. We believe, however limited and imperfect this proposal, that it is indeed operational and that it is an essential beginning to a more constructive life at McCarthy-Towne.

II. Background. Since the school's beginning the McC-T staff has debated the extent to which they should be involved in the school's operation. Last spring the organizational development weekend was a forum for the staff to express their approval/frustration/dissatisfaction with the organizational and administrative involvement that is expected of them. In its conclusions and recommendations the Task Force that planned and ran the weekend proposed and the staff created three new Task Forces:

1. One to explore ways of delegating responsibilities—to refine a model of working that is highly dependent on task forces.
2. One to develop leadership potential among the staff so that Task Forces, small groups, and large groups will have the leadership they need to achieve their purposes.
3. One to look at the issue of leadership in a larger

sense the need to coordinate the workings of the entire school. This group would spell out the work of an overviewer.

Because the end of the year was approaching, it was further proposed and agreed to that the work of Task Force #2 and Task Force #3 should be set aside and that the work of Task Force #1 deserved immediate attention.

By the time of the first meeting of the Task Force Parker had prepared a preliminary description of a Task Force model as well as some operational changes that might be needed to implement a Task Force model. The Task Force agreed to use Parker's model as a starting point.

The following proposal is the result of work done by the Task Force on June 12, August 18, August 22, and September 2.

ORGANIZATION DEVELOPMENT PROPOSAL

This proposal is in four interrelated parts:

Part I.   Discontinuation of the policy permitting an individual faculty member calling "An Important Question." Protection of individual and minority rights and views to be designed by a Task Force.

Part II.   Discontinuation of the policy necessitating the need for a quorum in order for a meeting to decide issues and the need for a majority vote when issues are decided. Instead, a meeting called with a minimum of one week's notice, and for which all proposals and information have been distributed at least one week in advance, may be held and an issue decided by a two thirds vote of the faculty present.

Part III. Discontinuation of all major decision making by the present system involving the entire faculty.

Instead, faculty meetings involving the entire faculty would be held the first Wednesday of each month. Six meetings (Sept., Oct., Dec., Feb., Apr., June) would be devoted to operational issues involving a faculty vote.

Four meetings (Nov., Jan., Mar., May) would be devoted to sharing ideas, discussing issues, and deciding broad philosophical and pedagogical goals and procedures. Parker would be responsible for coordinating the plans for these meetings.

Part IV. Description of Faculty Responsibilities and Organization.

GROUP A

Matters on Which Individual Staff Members May Act on Their Own

1. The individual teacher can decide the type of student evaluation used in his/her room.
2. Each teacher has the final say over the number and kind of volunteers in his/her classroom.
3. Materials and supplies for each room are selected by that teacher.
4. The individual teacher decides how he/she will utilize the support staff.
5. The classroom structure/schedule/routine is the responsibility of the teacher.

GROUP B

Matters on Which a Small Group May Decide on Their Own

1. Science money or money for one particular area may be turned over to a small group for decisions on its use.
2. After a program (e.g., gymnastics) has been agreed to a small group may decide on a plan for its implementation/coordination.
3. Small group(s) would be responsible for coordinating facilities and efficiently organizing all of the support staff services.
4. Small groups may plan and operate school events.
5. Whatever seasonal or special problems arise that are unrelated to management problems, a small group would decide on resolutions.
6. Screening for replacement or new position.
7. Small groups would make decisions on student placements.
8. Whenever necessary, small groups would create procedures to provide group and individual support to staff members.
9. Small groups could decide on appropriate workshops/seminars/evaluation for volunteers and student teachers.

GROUP C

Several Faculty Members to Decide

1. Use of Contracted Services Fund according to priorities & policies established in Grp. E. column.

2. Formal faculty evaluation.
3. Screening/Hiring
4. Faculty Assignments.
5. Budget priorities
6. Cross-School Curriculum priorities
7. Student and staff groupings
8. School-wide evaluation.
9. Parent and Community Communications
10. School-wide needs (plant, equipment, space).
11. Crisis crew—in emergency (time limited) situations Parker can call the Task Force (Crisis) to decide on an issue. This Task Force can have standing members or be chosen by Parker (depending on the wishes of each grade level grouping). This decision should be made by the end of September.
12. Special problem solving—created as a result of full staff recommendation.
13. Agenda Committee for 6 operational staff meetings.

GROUP D

Voting Faculty to Decide

1. School philosophy.
2. School goals
3. Program and Budget Priorities and Policies
4. Final Hiring/Firing and Hiring/Firing Policies
5. Curriculum and Program Policies
6. Roles and responsibilities each of us has, who does what.

GROUP E

Delegated to Individuals

1. Cur. Program Overview & Assessment.
2. Program & Personal Evaluation.
3. Program, Personnel & Facility Coordination.
4. Volunteer & Student-Teacher Operation.
5. Parent, System Comm. Communication & Representation.
6. Budget preparation & implementation.
7. Building operation:
   a) Maintenance
   b) Daily
   c) Long Range
8. Operation of non-school Services
   a) food
   b) transportation
9. Record keeping, Scheduling, and Communications
10. Long Range planning.

TASK FORCE—DEFINITION

1. Composition Group C: 1 or 2 people/grade level grouping (primary, intermediate, support staff)

Each grouping is responsible for seeing that they are represented on a Task Force.

Task Force must have minimum three people to function, maximum six people

Each Task Force must have chairperson and secretary

Task Force C must solicit concerns and ideas from all staff members. The request for concerns and ideas must be done in writing as well as orally.

2. Responsibilities of all Task Forces: Notice of each committee's progress must be posted for staff perusal. This should include what issues must be done in writing as well as orally. Minutes of meetings should be kept in a notebook in the office.

All decisions must be posted and presented at next full staff meeting.

Decisions must be made within the context of current policies.

ORGANIZATIONAL STRUCTURE OF THE OPEN DESIGN OFFICE, Architects and Planners, Cambridge, Massachusetts.

Analysis of the By-laws: the motivation preceeding them, their enactment in practice, and an evaluation.

August 1976, Joan Forrester Sprague

MOTIVATION	BYLAW	PRACTICE	EVALUATION
	I. *Basic Operating Principles*		
Distribution of assets should directly relate to work done. If no member earns from work done by others, (1) individual autonomy is reinforced (no one in the organization has monetary "control" over another), (2) flexible schedules are facilitated, (3) open boundaries for the organization are facilitated by lack of vested interest in profit.	No member takes profit from the office. All income is distributed as hourly payment for past or future work.	All income has been distributed as payment for past work, but never for future work. Some members have been drawn to profit-making ventures outside ODO.	Consistent, congruent and reinforcing of general goals—however does not provide incentive motivation to match conventional structure (draining energy from office.)
Autonomy requires that members be free to balance personal and work time commitments.	Members are free to make flexible schedules under Personal Time Commitment.	Some have kept rigid hours, needing this as discipline, most have not, all have benefitted from possibility for flexibility.	Technology of well-kept calendar, slack time and frequent rebalancing necessary. Energy focus outside of office allowed by flexibility may be a long-range liability to the office.

MOTIVATION	BYLAW	PRACTICE	EVALUATION
The organization exists in order to put the assets & skills of each individual at the disposal of others (to benefit from strengths and to fill in around weaknesses as identified by self and others.) For an integrated work product and process, authority and responsibility must be congruent.	The working relationship between members is non-hierarchical. Each member is in charge of her own work, and is encouraged to consult other members as resources. Final decisions regarding work are made by the member doing the work.	Each member has been in charge of own work, own decision-making, usually in consultation with others. Differences exist in terms of commitment to ODO, technical expertise, particular skills, interpersonal effectiveness, verbal effectiveness, confidence, etc. which may be perceived as hierarchy producing.	No measures or technology to define and evaluate what a "non-hierarchical-relationship" is, and therefore no method implied for testing. Self-perception of congruence between the bylaw and practice may differ from evaluation by the outside observer.
Sex role conditioning (and stereotyping) puts pressures on men and women to assume authority-dependency relationships. Self-definition and autonomy of members can be facilitated by absence of automatic (unconscious) sex role responses.	All members shall be women until such time that members vote to include men.	Still a future possibility. Discussed and not acted on at meetings.	May always remain a "future possibility," implying an attitude critical of separatism as an end in itself rather than a plan of action.
Autonomy is enforced by responsiveness of the organization to changing internal (member) needs, and changing external (environmental) pressures.	Procedures are in a state of evolution and are subject to adjustment and improvement.	Since by-laws were written (in Jan. 1975) no adjustment has been made in the written word, although some actual procedures, such as financial procedures, have varied.	Evolution to new norms appears to take place in practice. Conscious effort is required to explicate new norms and represent these in written adjustments to the bylaws. Bylaw does not specify the process for adjustment.

Although potential members may espouse support for organizational principles, a trial period provides data on the interpretation and acting-out of the principles in practice before members are committed to risks.

Joint risk-sharing is accomplished by risking payment for office time spent which is not specifically job related (and which is therefore not bringing money into the office.) This kind of risk time financed the office start-up. Necessary interface between an organization based on premises at variance with tradition and the external environment which reinforces tradition requires two categories of member where one would have been sufficient.

II. Membership

ODO members must approve prospective new members. A new member must work on an initial project in the office with a member, after which time she may become a full member. Those working in the office may be categorized as follows:

1. *Members:* both categories have similar privileges and responsibilities. Payment for work done which is not specifically job related is made quarterly or at the end of the fiscal year as the office can afford.
   a. *Partners*—all must sign partnership agreement, 50% must be licensed architects in Mass.
   b. *Risk-sharing consultants* —those who agree to same terms as partnership agreement.

Previous norm of "becoming a member overnight" sometimes proved extremely difficult, however, no new members have joined since bylaws were written, (perhaps coincidence or because work has been very slow.)

Members without conventional legal liability have acted (through conscious concern) to protect those with legal liability. No major liabilities have arisen; minor liabilities have been borne by working members.

Criteria for admission not spelled out, and incentives for admission not clarified. Is a new project always necessary for new membership? Not clear whether all or only working members must approve new member.

Commitment of members not completely articulated, i.e. Are risk-sharing members legally bound by their agreement if they are elsewhere on extended leave, and not in constant contact? Interpretation and assets may vary amongst individual members, and therefore acceptance of liability may vary.

MOTIVATION	BYLAW	PRACTICE	EVALUATION
Some special skills in addition to member's skills may be required, and ODO should be able to seek out persons with these special skills without requiring that these persons become members. However, since they are not sharing risks, they should be paid at a lower rate.	2. *Non-risk-sharing consultants:* paid bi-monthly or monthly at a rate fixed in advance for all work done for the office, including work which is not job related. Since these parameters establish a relationship between these and members which implies an employee employer relationship, these are used as infrequently as possible.	Some prefer security of dependency, or wish to have authority in decision-making without accepting responsibility for those decisions. ODO has had non-risk-sharing consultants primarily for services, such as secretarial.	Equality and autonomy may be of greater benefit and be more desirable to those with experience. For others, the protection of employment is an asset. Some choose a familiar mode in preference to shared risk.
	III. *Legal Requirements*		
Legal requirements must be met despite internal office workings which may be at variance.	Basic legal framework is a conventional partnership. At least 50% must be licensed by State law. In practice, by agreement, risk-sharing consultants have the same privileges and responsibilities as partners.	Legal requirements have been met.	Not implicitly consistent, congruent and reinforcing of goals. Alternative organization structure requires constant concern with the interface between external (traditional) and internal (innovative) systems which are at variance.
Maximal protection of partners and risk sharing consultants is desirable.	The office carries liability and office contents insurance.	Insurances have been discontinued since work-load (and risks) have diminished.	Need for insurance increases and decreases in relation to increased and decreased assets.

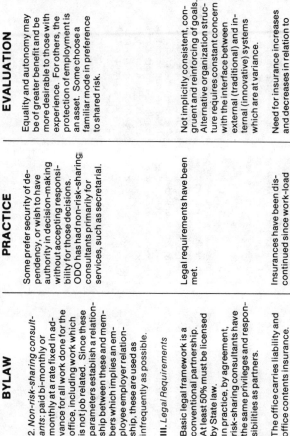

	IV. Financial Procedures		
Office charges should not be higher than, but not substantially lower than, conventional offices. Members should be explicit about charges to clients to involve the least possible risk to the office.	Unless otherwise agreed upon at an office meeting of members, the office charges each client a rate equal to 2½ times each member's hourly rate. Members may refuse to work for a client whom they believe is risky, and/or may require advance payment from the client.	At a time of scarce work, rates have been adjusted lower, and risky clients taken without advance payment.	Ideal is influenced by economic context.
Looking ahead in terms of risks the office is taking is the joint responsibility of all members, and therefore an agreed upon minimum balance is necessary.	The office must maintain sufficient funds in the bank to cover a minimum of three months overhead, which includes office rent, telephone, utilities, supplies, cleaning, etc.	Not honored after an arrangement was made to share office (and reduce expenses).	Conservatism of economic approach depends on members making decisions. (Does this mean that in times of poor economy, members with self-protective economic views will be occupied with work outside the office, and therefore working members making economic decisions will take higher risk?)

MOTIVATION	BYLAW	PRACTICE	EVALUATION
Variation of payment based on experience acknowledges the fact that a less experienced person will take longer to accomplish a task. Charges to clients are therefore equalized if rates of pay are tied to experience. However, a large gap between the lowest and highest rates of pay will tend to foster a hierarchical relationship between members.	The minimum rate of pay is somewhat higher than comparable salaries for less experienced members. The maximum is somewhat lower than what might be earned elsewhere for the most experienced members. Thus the fee structure has a 'leveling' tendency, with variation based on experience differential.	Those who earned at a higher rate were motivated to work less, those with low rate were motivated to work more. Specific varying rates of pay to members are decided by consensus at meetings and have been adjusted in response to new members.	Differences in rate of pay does not reflect non-hierarchical goal.
	V. *Office Meetings and Decision Making*		
The persons with responsibility on a project must have authority over their work to insure professional autonomy.	Job related issues, except for special financial considerations, are decided by those working on a job.	No member has interfered with another member's project or work, unless explicitly asked for suggestions.	Some errors were made that might have been avoided with a more explicit control system. Are benefits of creative work based in autonomy a tradeoff for possible errors? Is a control system more error-free, or are some errors always inevitable?

Sharing of information relating to joint concerns is necessary if joint responsibility is expected. The benefit o·seeing and analyzing the pro·lem from a variety of perspectives encourages a creative process. Disclosure of all information relevant or helpful for members and projects is seen a benefiting the entire group. Talking through differences until agreement is reached encourages group support for the decision. (It is "owned" by all.)

ODO members meet regularly once a week to settle questions of office policy and management. Matters to be discussed and settled include new members, acceptance or rejection of jobs, fees, time scheduling, teaching activities, promotion and project related issues requested by member(s) working on that project. Questions are decided by consensus. A formal vote has never been necessary.

Meetings are rarely long enough and are difficult to schedule. Some members have monopolized meetings by personality, others hardly speak. Disclosure has been encouraged, but personality differences make maximally open sharing difficult. Decisions always made by consensus.

Group meeting and consensus decision making requires maximal number of 6-8, otherwise there is too much data to process and too many people to hear out. No technology for testing whether all have been heard, since differences in personality provide unequal quantity of data from each member.

MOTIVATION	BYLAW	PRACTICE	EVALUATION
	VI. *New Projects and Job Responsibilities*		
Members must agree on the kind of work and clients ODO has, and they must be self-initiating job responsibilities.	All partners and risk sharing members must approve new jobs. Jobs coming to the office (except for a job directed to a specific person by the client) will be handled by the person whose time, money requirements and interests are deemed best suited to the job by office consensus.	Approval by all members has not always been sought. Job assignments have been made by members volunteering for projects or tasks, and balancing these interests. Self-interest at the expense of other members and/or the office is not an office norm.	Approval is not consistent with the autonomy principle. If a member wishes to work on a project, and if it presents no special risk, what are criteria for rejection? Should these criteria for rejection be explicit, so that approval is not necessary? Is office norm of concern for others and backing away from self-interest a characteristic of those attracted to the organization, in turn also enhanced by organization norms? Is the characteristic rooted in sex role conditioning?
The client must have a personal contact in the office who is the responsible ODO representative.	At least one person must take personal responsibility for the progress of each job.	All members have had primary responsibility for projects.	Shared responsibility of office facilitates distribution of job responsibilities to individuals.

ODO does not wish to constrain outside opportunities for members, but information regarding plans must be shared in order for the office to plan ahead effectively.	Although members are expected to make efforts to obtain business for the office, members may take on individual projects outside the office with the advance consent of other members.	All members have not made efforts to obtain business for ODO. Some have directed their energy outside the office to insure greater profit, short-range gains, and more individual financial security.	Not clear if this is a factor of the economic depression in building, or if the ODO organization structure implies intrinsically that energy will be directed outward from the organization.
	VII. *Personal Time Commitment*		
In order to balance work-hours available with work hours required by office projects, and to balance work needed by ODO members with work available, a range of total work-hours (from minimum to maximum possible) must be known for planning.	A month before the beginning of each quarter year, each partner and consultant member must state minimum optimum, and maximum hour work loads to fit her time schedule and financial needs. She may indicate the days and amount of time she wishes to work. Members are expected to fulfill these estimates if work is available.	Time estimates are not always dependable, based on inaccurate estimation by members.	Provided relatively effective technology for balancing time and work, providing slack time factor is used to balance poor time estimations.

MOTIVATION

Risk time should be spread in proportion to earnings by an explicit technology in order to clarify the responsibility of partners and risk-sharing members, and to insure that sufficient time is spent on work that is not job related.

BYLAW

Time equalling at least one third of each members project time is spent on work which is not related to any specific job. This work may include promotion, meetings, library, bookkeeping and minimal secretarial work. (Most secretarial and clerical jobs are done by outside consultants.) Members payment for this work is made annually in proportion to total job time, and in proportion to available funds.

PRACTICE

Some members have spent a great deal of risk time compared to others, and this difference has provided a potential for dissension and conflict. However, proportions have been adjusted by ad hoc changes in the technology for figuring payment. This technology has not been recorded as a norm.

EVALUATION

Most difficult to evaluate, since this risk-sharing time insures the continuity of ODO, and is difficult to generate in the necessary quantities for effective promotion at times of economic slump. (Less projec- related work in the office causes less risk time to be available when the need for this time to secure additional work is most necessary. However, the organization struc- ture permits a response to the economic slump by shrinking overhead costs, obviating the danger of bankruptcy which may be connected to fixed overhead.)

Index

226

228